DAILY
MEDITATIONS

Front cover: Getty images – Crocus (close-up)
Frank Krahmer

© Copyright Prosveta S.A. 2007. All rights reserved for all countries. No part of this publication may be reproduced, translated, adapted, stored in a retrieval system or transmitted, whether privately or otherwise, in any form or by any means, electronic, mechanical, photocopying, audio-visual or otherwise, without the prior permission of author and publishers (Law of March 1957 revised).

Prosveta S.A – B.P.12 – 83601 Fréjus CEDEX (France)

ISBN 978-2-85566-944-1

original edition: ISBN 978-2-85566-943-4

Omraam Mikhaël Aïvanhov

DAILY
MEDITATIONS

2008

PROSVETA

I

Every morning, before you do anything else, you must give yourself a few quiet moments of reflection so as to begin your day in peace and harmony, and unite yourself to the Creator by dedicating the new day to Him through prayer, meditation.

It is the beginning that is all-important, for it is then, at the beginning, that new forces are set in motion and given direction. If we want to act wisely and well, we have to begin by casting some light on the situation. You do not look for something or start work in the dark; you start by lighting a lamp so that you can see what you are doing. And you can apply the same principle to every area in life: in order to know what to do and how to do it, you have to switch on the light – in other words, to concentrate and look into yourself. Without this light you will wander in all directions and knock on many different doors, and you will never achieve anything worthwhile.

Our days follow the direction that we give to our first thoughts in the morning, for, depending on whether we are mindful or not, we either clear the way ahead or litter it with all kinds of useless and even dangerous debris. Disciples of initiatic science know how to begin the day so that it may be fruitful and rich in God's grace, and so that they may share that grace with those around them. They understand how important it is to begin the day with one fundamental thought around which all the other thoughts of the day may revolve.

If you keep your sights fixed on a definite goal, a clear orientation, an ideal, all your activities will gradually organize themselves and fall into line in such a way as to contribute to the realization of that ideal. Even the negative or alien thoughts or feelings that attempt to infiltrate you will be deflected and put at the service of the divine world. Yes, even they will be forced to follow the direction you have chosen. In this way, thanks to the fundamental thought that you place in your head and your heart first thing in the morning, your whole day will be recorded in the book of life.

And, since everything we do is recorded, once you have lived one glorious day, one day of eternal life, not only will that day be recorded, not only will it never die, but it will endeavor to get the days that follow to imitate it. Try to live just one day as well as you possibly can, therefore, and it will influence all your days: it will persuade them to listen to its testimony and follow its example, so as to be well balanced, orderly, and harmonious.

Omraam Mikhaël Aïvanhov

GLOSSARY

Definitions of terms as used by the Master Omraam Mikhaël Aïvanhov:

Brotherhood: a collectivity governed by a truly cohesive spirit, in which each individual works consciously for the good of all.

Collectivity: a group of people, usually quite extensive, united by a common interest, a common organization or common sentiments, or living in the same place or country.

Disinterestedness: altruism, the absence of bias motivated by interest or advantage. This is a central part of the Master's philosophy.

Psychic: (as in 'psychic life / world / bodies, etc.') refers not to mediumship but to a human being's subtle energy beyond the physical, i.e. heart, mind, soul and spirit.

Spiritualist: refers to anyone who looks at things from a spiritual point of view, whose philosophy of life is based on belief in a spiritual reality.

1 January

On the first day of this New Year, I wish you all the blessings of heaven.

May your body be healthy and vigorous, your heart be filled with pure, spiritual joy, your intellect receive true light to make your path clear, your soul become a conductor for divine love, and your spirit, freed from its fetters, escape from all physical and psychic prisons.

May you remain linked to the great hierarchy of celestial beings, so you can work with them for the establishment of the kingdom of God on earth.

And finally, may you be capable of overcoming each obstacle that arises, so each day may be an opportunity to glorify the Creator

2 January

Whatever inadequacies we may appear to have, in reality we possess everything we need to draw closer every day to a state of holiness, that state of purity and light which is an attribute of God himself, according to the book of *Revelations,* where the Seraphim that stand before the throne repeat without ceasing, *'Holy, holy, holy, the Lord God the Almighty.'*

But God has equipped us so thoroughly that he has even given us elements that resist holiness. We must work to transform these elements, for that is how we will attain true holiness.

Holiness is a state that is reached in full consciousness. What advantage would there be in walking along the path of goodness like a robot, without knowing either why or how we were progressing? Before we can appreciate the light, we must have overcome darkness, for our knowledge of light is enriched by our knowledge of darkness.

3 January

On the physical plane, people exist as separate, individual beings, and their lives do not directly affect the lives of others. To all appearances, your suffering or joy is not their suffering or joy. If you persist in eating indigestible food, you will damage your own stomach, not theirs. But above, on the subtle planes, there are no barriers between beings, and all our inner states affect others. Yes, for above there exists only one being, the cosmic Man who is a synthesis of all beings.

We live in cosmic Man, in fact we are this cosmic Man, and no creature exists as a separate entity. In consequence, we have the moral law that we cannot do good or evil to others without also doing it to ourselves. Perhaps, at face value, this doesn't make much sense? Well, on the contrary, it makes a great deal of sense, for within the cosmic Man we are one.

4 January

Do you aspire to inner peace? Few things are as difficult to obtain. But work on the idea of loving, of doing good, of forgiving others and bringing harmony everywhere you go. The time will come when this idea becomes so powerful it will impregnate all your cells, and they will begin to vibrate in unison with it. And then peace will gradually steal its way into you, and it will never leave you again.

Of course, life on earth is such that it's impossible for you not to be troubled by events from time to time. But they will only make a few ripples on the surface; deep down, you will always feel that peace reigns within you.

5 January

Each day you must consecrate your life to heaven, saying: 'O sublime Spirits, I believe only in you, for you alone are faithful and true. So I give you my life; do with me as you will, guide me, enlighten me, strengthen me, manifest yourselves through me.'

Are you wondering how you can give your life to heaven? This is very simple: by leaving the lower world of disorder and darkness in order to enter the higher world of harmony and light. For, contrary to what some people believe, you cannot live in the gutter and in heaven at the same time. They live a life of debauchery but imagine that the Deity will present itself to them all the same. But no, heaven is closed to people like that! When you immerse yourself in certain impassioned states, you can no longer gain access to heavenly regions; they remain closed. In order to be accepted, you have to detach yourself, to 'die' in the initiatic sense of the word. That is what it means to give your life to heaven.

6 January

Love manifests throughout the universe. When you wake up in the morning and open your eyes to the world, don't you feel you are already receiving love? All this life coming to you from heaven and earth is love, a love that springs forth from the divine Source. Give thanks, and try to fill yourself with this love.

The day you learn to receive this love, not only will you feel fulfilled but everywhere you go you will lavish your abundant riches on those around you. And how could those who receive these riches not love you? They will love you because you ask for nothing; you simply give. Will you finally accept that only this way of understanding and expressing love will actually bring you love?

7 January

Technical progress has made life more comfortable, but be wary of comfort. You will perhaps not like this idea, but the truth is comfort paralyses intelligence, whereas the lack of comfort stimulates it; it stimulates the need to create. Most of humanity's great masterpieces have been created in discomfort. 'And isn't anyone creating masterpieces anymore?' you will ask. Of course they are, only the masterpieces in our times are no longer masterpieces of art or philosophy but extremely sophisticated machines and appliances, masterpieces of technology. These machines and appliances are the most remarkable achievements of our time, and it's true, you can't help but admire them. But these laudable achievements are in the process of paralysing and chloroforming human beings.

We are on earth in order to develop. And developing ourselves means exercising the power of spirit over matter: not only the matter outside us but especially that within us. And we will only know how to control external matter intelligently when we have learnt to control our inner matter; otherwise we will be crushed.

8 January

How many mystics have suffered from feeling abandoned by God! In reality, God didn't abandon them; it was they who failed to remain conscious of his presence. God never abandons us; it is within our own consciousness that these changes take place. Of course, it is difficult to remain permanently convinced and to sense constantly that we are inhabited by the divine presence, but this is what we must work towards; we must make our entire being a temple to the supreme Being. Yes, not even a palace, but a temple. Of course, if you manage to make a palace of your inner being, it's a start, but a palace lacks that element of consecration found in a temple.

God will enter those who have succeeded in making themselves a temple, and he will never leave them again: the supreme Being does not leave a sanctuary that has been dedicated to himself, where he continues to be worshipped in purity and light.

9 January

We breathe, and our respiration is the reflection of an immense cosmic respiration, that of God himself. God breathes in and out… He breathes out, and a new universe appears. He breathes in, and everything disappears and merges into him.

Man breathes in and out eighteen times a minute, whereas it is impossible to calculate how many millions of years it takes for cosmic inhalation and exhalation. The life of human beings begins with their first breath and ends with their last. And between these two moments, life is nothing other than an uninterrupted succession of inhalations and exhalations. It is for us to find the deeper meaning of this.

10 January

Light is the matter of creation, and, although it is diffused everywhere throughout space and impregnates everything, humans do not see it. They do not sense it, because they are not yet spiritually developed enough to perceive such a subtle reality; they still have a great deal of work to do in this respect. Those who habitually concentrate on light refine their perceptions to such an extent they begin not only to sense it but to attract it to themselves.

You say you do not know what subjects to meditate on? Concentrate on the light, feel that you are attracting it, bringing it into your whole being, and then all the old particles of your body will be gradually replaced with new, pure, luminous particles. Never stop seeking the light; it is the only thing capable of restoring perfect harmony within you. By doing this exercise you are working for your salvation.

11 January

Only experience can give us access to the reality of the divine world. The books we read on this subject will give us a few glimmers of light and a general sense of direction, but that is not enough. We then need to be able to go elsewhere for instruction, to live something elsewhere. This journey to somewhere else, which mystics call ecstasy, takes place when a being is projected out of their body.

True knowledge, that which becomes flesh and bone within us, is only truly acquired if we succeed in rising to those regions where all of creation and all creatures have their origin. The great founders of religion received their inspiration from above. According to tradition, they were taught by the archangels; it is said that Metatron taught Moses, the archangel Gabriel taught Mohammed, and so on, which is a way of saying true knowledge comes from above and we must seek it above. To all those who are capable of rising to the higher regions of consciousness, the same truths are revealed. The forms and expressions are different, but the principles are the same.

12 January

A lyre is not just a musical instrument invented, according to Greek legend, by the god Hermes. It symbolizes the human being, with each string corresponding to one of their bodies. But most humans are content to make only one string vibrate: their physical body. They do not bother much with the other strings: the astral, mental, causal, buddhic and atmic bodies,* which is why the music they make is so pitiful!

The disciples of an initiatic school study the nature and properties of each string, of each body, and they try to develop them. These exercises concern the whole person and, therefore, presuppose a new way of life that takes into account the least activities of everyday life, for their aim is to achieve a state where there is no longer any dissonance between the physical body, heart, intellect, will, soul and spirit. Those who have understood the profound symbolism of the lyre will themselves become a lyre, vibrating in unison with the entire cosmos, and they will be received amongst the sons and daughters of heaven.

* See note and diagram p. 376-377.

13 January

It can happen to anyone, that feeling as if you're crossing an arid desert inside yourself. You no longer feel any zest for life or desire to do anything; everything has become insipid, alien and empty. This is the most dreadful state a human being can fall into. The worst thing that can happen is not to encounter failure, become ill or lose all your money but to find you no longer have any love, ardour or faith, that you have lost the meaning of life. So you must think about preparing within yourself the essential elements you need to face this type of situation.

Each difficulty has a specific solution; this solution could be light or will or humility or purity or love… That is why the disciples of a spiritual teaching must neglect nothing, omit nothing, so they can triumph over all the obstacles that, sooner or later, will be found on their path. Even if they do not need certain elements today, that is no reason for them not to try to acquire them, for they will need them sooner or later.

14 January

'I am the way, and the truth, and the life', said Jesus. In order to interpret his idea correctly, we must assimilate these three words and re-form them into a unity. And how can we do that? With the help of the image of a river. At the source of a river there is a spring: that is truth. From the spring flows water, which is life. And gradually over time, water erodes a path, which is the way. Do you know why I based my philosophy on the three words love, wisdom and truth? It is because they are linked to Jesus' words, *'I am the way, and the truth, and the life.'*

To begin with, then, there is the source (truth); from this source flows life (love), and the riverbed, or the path this water takes for its descent, is wisdom. Water comes from above, and it descends to bring us life. But to drink it in all its purity, we must go to seek it at the source. Water descends, but we will only receive all its blessings if, through prayer and meditation, we rise to the divine Source.

15 January

How often do you hear, 'If God existed, he wouldn't allow so many injustices to be committed.' If we wish to understand God's patience, we must never lose sight of the law of cause and effect, one of the fundamental laws of creation. There is no cause without effect anywhere in the universe; every act and every element is the consequence of a cause. It is only the brevity of life that prevents human beings from having the correct viewpoint and the correct understanding of events; the causes and consequences escape them. That is why they are impatient.

Patience is a virtue that is acquired through an awareness of the continuance of life. As long as people are unable to take a long-term view, they are impatient and draw hasty conclusions, for they see only aberrations and injustice everywhere. Those, on the other hand, who are capable of seeing how the law of cause and effect works will notice that everything is just and everything has meaning.

16 January

The earth is the sphere of all material realizations. On the one hand, this is greatly encouraging, but at the same time it is very dangerous, since evil as well as good is materialized. There are regions in the universe where evil has no hold, but on earth everything has the right to be realized; you have to grasp this. That is why, in the face of all the crime being committed and all the misfortune striking humanity, it is no use asking yourself, 'But how can God allow such things to happen?' It is not a question of God's permission; it is simply the nature of things. It is like that because we are on earth, and on earth both good and evil can find the conditions they need for realization.

So, for good as for evil, we must develop patience: the patience to endure the schemes of evil, which make us suffer, and the patience to wait for the realization of the good things we are hoping and working for.

17 January

Contrary to what is generally believed, in order to receive we must first give. It is true you cannot give if you do not already possess something, and if you have received nothing you cannot possess anything. But it is a question of knowing from where and from whom to receive.

Yet, instead of drawing their needs from the invisible world, most humans turn to other human beings, and that's how they gradually take everything the others have: not only their money and possessions but also their energy, ideas and feelings… You could even say that lovers are the greatest thieves alive! And as there are nothing but love stories everywhere, in poetry and novels, and at the theatre and cinema, that means there are only stories about thieves: yes, it's true, it's all about who will succeed in stealing the heart, attention and time of another. If you observe and reflect on this, you will notice that, on the psychic plane as on the physical plane, people do nothing but steal.

18 January

The knowledge we possess falls into two categories: that which is truly ours, because we have really tasted it and lived it, and that which is in some way foreign to us, because it remains theoretical book knowledge. Those content to limit themselves to theoretical knowledge will return in their next life as ignorant and as limited as they would if they had never learnt anything. Whereas the most humble, insignificant men and women, who have worked to put into practice what they have learnt in the realm of virtues, will return with faculties that enable them to manifest as truly wise and intelligent beings.

Knowledge that you have put into practice, made part of your life, will remain in your possession for ever: you will take it with you to whatever planet you go to live on in the future. But all your theoretical knowledge, which, in fact, is only borrowed knowledge, will be erased and lost to you.

19 January

People occasionally ask me, in connection with family members or for themselves for the future, whether it is better to bury a dead person or have them cremated. It is difficult to reply categorically to such a question.

For most humans, burial is certainly preferable, because their soul needs a great deal of time to leave the physical body: they were so attached to material possessions and earthly pleasures that their soul remains there, restlessly drifting around their body. Some won't even have believed in life after death, so now they don't understand where they are. They need entities from the invisible world to enlighten and guide them. So, if their body is burnt after their death, they are left disoriented by the brutal separation of their body and soul. On the other hand, very spiritual beings, who have learnt all their life to detach themselves from matter, can be cremated: fire helps them to cut all links with their physical body more quickly. But those who conduct such a cremation must possess a certain spiritual knowledge, so as to be conscious of what they are doing. The body of a human being, even when dead, must not be burnt as though it were a piece of old furniture.

20 January

The rituals prescribed by religions are only forms. These forms are, of course, useful but only to the extent that the believer is capable of bringing life to them, making them meaningful.

The most important ritual for Christians is communion. But it is only beneficial for them to receive the host and wine if they have learnt to commune with the Creator in a greater, more profound way, through the simple acts of everyday life: eating, drinking, walking, breathing, looking, listening, sleeping, loving and working. Yes, it's true: when we breathe, when we sleep, when we contemplate nature, the mountains, the sea, the sun and the stars, we are able to live magnificent states of consciousness which are a form of communion. In fact, it is this communion which then gives meaning to Christian communion.

21 January

We will not live on earth or in our physical body for all eternity. That is why, in our psychic, spiritual life we must never be defeated by material conditions but must always find a way for the spirit to triumph. Matter, with all the difficulties it presents, has been given to us as a stimulus for the spirit, and by 'matter' we must understand not only the physical body but equally our psychic world, which is also a type of matter; it may be less opaque than the matter of the physical world, but it is matter all the same. So, you must no longer say, 'I can't do anything; look at all these obstacles stopping me!' You think that stating this fact proves you're right, for 'that's how things are', but there are other facts you have overlooked. You give in to a material, objective reality. But if you know how to act, another reality, which is every bit as real, will have the last word: divine Reality.

22 January

Alchemists have described the preparation of the philosopher's stone as 'woman's work and child's play'. We must understand that this refers to very specific play and work, relating to the role and vocation of the masculine and feminine principles. The true task of woman is one that man is incapable of performing: to carry her child in the womb and bring it into the world. Whereas 'child's play' is the domain of man: his role is 'to play' so that the woman is given this seed to carry and bring to maturity.

So those who wish to fathom the secret of the philosopher's stone must understand the elements and processes that are set in motion when a man and woman conceive a child, and then, once the child is conceived, they must understand how it is formed in its mother's womb. The preparation of the philosopher's stone obeys the same laws as conception and gestation, because the same laws govern the different kingdoms of creation.

23 January

Why is it so difficult for humans to live together? It is because they have absolutely no consideration for each other, no respect. That is why the collective life is a wonderful opportunity to develop and expand one's consciousness. Those who live a solitary life can be selfish and capricious; there is no one for whom they have to make the effort to monitor and improve their behaviour. But once they start dealing with others, what an effort they have to make!

The proof of a human being's evolution is how conscious they are of belonging to a whole, much greater than themselves, whose harmony they are careful not to disturb by their activity, thoughts, feelings and inner noise. You will ask, 'What do you mean by inner noise?' Yes, all noise is the result of dissonance, and the noise we make inwardly, with our feelings, our trauma and rebellion, troubles the psychic atmosphere. Those who make this noise do not know they are also hurting themselves, for one day this noise will appear within them in the form of psychic disturbances or even physical illness.

24 January

The few minutes of prayer and meditation we have before meals create the conditions needed for eating to become a sacred act. So, why are even Christians gradually losing this habit? But, whether or not you are a Christian, try to understand that it is important to meditate for a moment before you eat, so as to be fully conscious of the importance of the gestures you are about to make and to be in control of them throughout the meal.

Control of our gestures is one of the conditions for the control of our thoughts and feelings. So, before each meal, remain silent for a few seconds; immerse yourself in the awareness of how important, even indispensable, to life this act of eating is. Be respectful of your food, and your gestures will be imbued with a suppleness, a harmony, a gentleness and an extraordinary love that will reflect on you. And then with what ease you will carry out your everyday tasks!

25 January

You constantly meet men and women who are worried and unhappy. What means do you have to help them? You will sympathize and suffer with them… But even if they are touched to see you are not indifferent to their misfortune, what will your compassion really bring them?

You can only help others if you acquire the habit of travelling, every day, to a country where riches abound – the riches of love, light and joy. This country is the divine world. How can those who are poor, worried and joyless help others? You must go to God to find total nourishment for your heart and soul. Then you will be able to distribute this to those around you and, by your example, you will teach others to do the same.

26 January

Within the family and within society, every one must carry out tasks and play roles, conscious of their responsibilities. But at the same time, they must never forget that everything in this world passes, and these roles are only exercises that cosmic Intelligence has provided for humans as a stimulus for them to perfect themselves. In this sense, you can say the earth is both a school and a stage at the same time. We must apply ourselves to our 'exercises' and do them as well as we can but, on the other hand, not take our role too seriously, in other words, not cling to it as though nothing more important existed and this situation was going to last forever.

What would people say of an actor who continued to act like King Lear, Napoleon or Sheherazade after he had left the stage? Well, that is what humans tend to do, especially those who have honorary positions: they identify with their task, they forget they are on the scene for very little time. But initiates never forget. They are conscious that their passage on earth and the role they have to play there are of a fleeting nature. That is why they always act with lucidity, moderation and disinterestedness.

27 January

Through meditation and prayer we learn to communicate with the higher regions and project the subtlest part of our soul towards heaven, so that on its return it may bring us new, more spiritual elements we did not possess before. And then, instead of eternally repeating the same faults, the same erroneous behaviour or the same mediocrity, we will succeed in surpassing ourselves.

If animals evolve very little, it is because they are deprived of this projective faculty that humans possess. For thousands of years, they have been reproducing identical copies of themselves, and if they evolve at all it is thanks to their contact with humans. Whereas human beings, through the power they have to project themselves into divine regions, attract purer, more luminous elements to themselves, and in this way they manage to surpass themselves, to recreate themselves and accomplish tremendous works. That is what we call evolution.

28 January

Do not commit yourself to a relationship simply because you like someone, or, if you do, be aware of what to expect. For there will be no use in complaining to everyone afterwards about this or that person, saying, 'He deceived me' or 'She cheated on me. I didn't think she was capable of doing that to me.'

Do you want to love and be loved? It's completely normal! But at least know how to choose your relationships and especially how to sustain them. In order to sustain them, pay particular attention to what you say. Sometimes a few negative words are enough to destroy years of amicable relations. Pay scrupulous attention to the slightest thing you say, for each and every word leaves traces.

29 January

You have become used to putting up with your inner states, even the most negative ones. Why is that? When you sense a psychic difficulty, concentrate your thoughts on it; impregnate it with light and warmth. In that way, you will manage to harmonize the particles of your astral and mental bodies*, and a few minutes afterwards you will notice an improvement.

Thought is still an unknown power, but if you want to obtain results try to concentrate your thought so that it penetrates your psychic organism, where it will neutralize the negative elements. Mental concentration is one of the great rules of spiritual life. Put it into practice, and you will discover its effectiveness.

* See note and diagram p. 376-377.

30 January

'Be perfect as your heavenly Father is perfect'. It was two thousand years ago that Jesus said this, but have Christians really tried to attain even a little of their heavenly Father's perfection? They always prove to be greedy, weak, jealous, resentful, angry and sensual. This shows that the teaching they have been given since then is not enough to change them; they need something more. Some of you will say, 'But what do you mean? We have everything; it's all in the Gospels!' Yes, of course, but have you understood the Gospels? Have you been shown the depth of the truths they contain? No, people are happy with a few snatches of verses they have often been unable to interpret correctly.

Everything is in the Gospels, it's true, but there is not much in Christians' heads, as they haven't received the explanations they need or the methods to apply them.

31 January

As they do not know very much, most people think they can say almost anything on the subject of spirituality and spiritualists. No, no! If someone has absolutely no light in his face, it is clear he is spiritually under-nourished, because he hasn't known which inner restaurant to go into to nourish himself. You may say, 'Yes, but if he prays, if he meditates, if he's honest, charitable and modest, if he's faithful to his wife…' He may be all of that, but if no clarity emanates from him it is because he does not know how to feed his inner self. How is it that none of his virtues show on his face?

But then I meet a radiant being. Whatever people say about him, I think, 'Here is someone who has the secret of spiritual life, and I want to learn this secret from him, for he is a sun, a flowing spring!'

1 February

Learn to appreciate a truth for itself without worrying about the social position of those speaking to you or the letters after their name. For each truth is valid in itself, and it remains valid irrespective of whose mouth it comes from, just as a gold coin remains gold no matter whose pocket it is found in. Of course, a gold coin received from a king's hand has special value for you, for your vanity is flattered. Even though it doesn't contain a milligram more gold, you can say, 'The king gave it to me!' And you may even be able to sell it for more, since items and furniture that have belonged to people of renown get sold for a higher price. But that's just snobbery.

A truth, whether it is scientific, philosophical or spiritual, has its own value. If you are evolved enough not to limit your attention to form, you will be as attentive to the truth that's told you by someone unknown as by someone famous.

2 February

Take a piece of sulphur: it is hard, solid. Now, heat it: it becomes soft, almost liquid. But if you continue to heat it, it will harden again. It is exceptional for a chemical substance to become solid again once it has softened, and it is interesting to find the correspondences between this phenomenon and our psychic life.

In alchemical science, sulphur and mercury represent the two principles, masculine and feminine, in other words the intellect and heart. So, in sulphur's transformation through the effects of heat, we see the different phases through which the human intellect passes when confronted with the question of religion and faith. Those whose intellect is undeveloped believe everything they are taught by religion without any discernment; they have what we call 'blind faith'. But once they become more educated, they develop their critical faculty, and then doubt gradually creeps in, their convictions weaken and they lose their faith. However, if they continue their education and start to think more deeply about things, they will regain their faith, true faith, an unshakeable faith that is based on knowledge.

3 February

Human beings are on earth to work; and when I say work, I mean to work first on themselves, to make the effort to transcend their limitations, to surpass themselves. People go off to work every day, of course, but their efforts in this respect are mainly aimed at ensuring their livelihood, their well-being and their material security. They are not particularly prepared for the mental work that would make them master of all situations. They count on an easy existence where nothing painful or unfortunate will ever happen to them. The Lord himself must protect them, give them peace of mind and good health; that is even why they pray to him. As for non-believers, they expect to be assisted and protected by society.

But no, humans must understand they will never be totally protected or beyond harm's reach. They are on earth to learn and develop, and their difficulties and ordeals are there precisely in order to get them to do this; there is no escape. So, instead of running in all directions with their demands, protests and complaints, each one must do some inner work, for they will find the remedies, comfort and hope they need within themselves first.

4 February

It is time for believers of all religions to stop attacking each other and brandishing their sacred books as being the sole guardians of God's word. For that is wrong, yes, wrong and ridiculous, and true faith gains nothing by these quarrels. Why are believers of all religions still told it was God himself who spoke to the prophets and that their 'sacred' texts contain only eternal truths? All the holy books are still only fragments, incomplete, imperfect copies of the only great book that was truly written by God: the universe, which also includes the human being, created in the image of the universe.

Some people will accuse me of sacrilege, of heresy. Well, let them yell as much as they like. It is only the ignorant that could possibly be indignant, for they do not know how God envisaged the universe and humans. Even if the sacred books were inspired by heaven – and they certainly were – they do not solely contain truths that are irrefutable and for all time.

5 February

Even if it is impossible for them to be completely unaware of the fact, it is better for children of very rich families not to know the extent of the fortune they will one day inherit. Children who count on their future inheritance believe they are naturally exempt from having to make any effort or from learning to get by on their own. They become lazy, capricious and good for nothing. And that is how the parents' fortune is the cause of their children's moral decline. Parents should therefore leave their children in ignorance of their future inheritance for as long as possible. Once they have acquired good work habits and self-control, there will be no danger in them being made aware of it.

How does the Lord act with humans? As he is the greatest of all teachers, the greatest pedagogue, he does not immediately show them the inheritance that awaits them in the heavenly mansions on high. So, believing themselves poor and wretched, they work and sweat. And when, after all their tears and suffering, they prove themselves worthy of their inheritance, their heavenly Father will reveal all the treasures he has amassed for them.

6 February

The invisible world is just like the visible world: it is inhabited by some extremely evolved creatures, luminous entities, pure and true, but also by others that are inclined to deceive humans so as to harm them. Unfortunately, it is often the latter that are present at spiritualist séances. Yes, it's true; do you really imagine that the most evolved entities are at the beck and call of the first person to call themselves a medium, or that they waste their time satisfying the curiosity and desires of those who take part in séances?

Of course, you are free to feed on illusions, but the truth is plain: the entities that respond to the call of mediums are often larvae of the lower astral plane, elementals, and not those the mediums believe they have called. Do you wish to call up spirits? Be aware, at least, that the quality and accuracy of their messages depends on your degree of evolution and that of the medium. Human beings attract either luminous or dark entities, depending on the quality of their inner life.

7 February

Woman's vocation is to be the educator of man. By her thoughts, feelings and her attitude she can encourage him to accomplish the noblest of acts. Man asks only to be uplifted and inspired by her. That is why, as long as women do not have this ideal, as long as they think only of their desires and pleasures, they will not fulfil their true vocation. You will say, 'But woman is so much weaker and more delicate than man! How can she oppose him?' She does not need to oppose him. Certain attitudes, certain forms of expression are more effective than all the words and gestures you could make. And woman has another means of educating man: by educating her sons, and these sons will respect women all their life because of their mother. Yes, through the daily influence they can have over their sons, mothers are capable of creating upright, noble and generous characters.

8 February

All of nature – mountains, rivers, trees, crystals, metals, all living beings, even human beings – is nothing other than numbers incarnated. If you study this question in depth, you will find that nothing exists apart from numbers. Everything is number; nature and the whole universe are built upon numbers, which form an indestructible, geometric framework similar to the skeleton.

So mathematics is abstract only at the level of principles; in the created world it takes on flesh and bone. For the moment, mathematicians work without knowing how the results of their calculations correspond to reality. One day, they will discover that all the physical, psychic and cosmic processes are there, all explained by numbers and their different combinations.

9 February

When they are confronted with difficulties, many people end up saying to themselves, 'Why break my neck looking for a solution? From now on, things can simply take their course.' Well, that's how you court failure. Thought is an instrument. Yes, the capacity to think, reason and reflect about every situation is the best thing that God has given us. Why would anyone want to get rid of it? It would be just like walking blindfold on the edge of a precipice. Of course, it is difficult to think, especially to think well, but it is the only way to evolve.

Actually, there are two ways of thinking: one that brings grief and suffering because you have not learnt to reflect and one that, on the contrary, brings peace and joy. Analyse yourself, and you will notice this. So, try to limit your thoughts to those that will help to keep you upright.

10 February

It is not enough for an initiatic teaching to inform you of the existence of the different subtle bodies you have beyond your physical body. It must give you criteria for discerning the quality of your states of consciousness and their corresponding thoughts and emotions. And it must also give you methods to develop your spiritual organs, which will enable you to cross the region of illusory perceptions and reach the regions of soul and spirit with assurance.

After much work and many exercises, the day will come when you will see the realities of the psychic and spiritual world with the same clarity, accuracy and precision as you see the realities of the physical plane. And that is when you will contemplate true life; you will see all things as a whole, and when you have to explain or describe them you will present the exact truth.

11 February

When you love someone, it is God that loves them through you. So, by loving them, you experience the love of God. That is why the act of loving can be just as fulfilling as that of being loved, in fact, even more so.

You have certainly already felt this love. It visited you, but then it went away… and that is how it will always be until love finds a permanent dwelling place and nourishment within you. For it eats a great deal! So, next time it comes to visit, try to reflect on the circumstances of its coming, so you are able to summon it again, for it is you, consciously or not, who provide the favourable conditions it needs. Love enters where there is purity, the purity symbolized by the transparency of a crystal, and if it finds impurity it leaves again. So you see, this is a very serious question; think about it instead of complaining of being alone and abandoned. You can never lose the love that lives within you. If you feel abandoned, it means you, yourself, no longer love.

12 February

Why does the church maintain Christians in their illusions with promises that will never be realized? They are ill, weak and poor, both physically and spiritually... But never mind, the church consoles them by telling them, 'Don't worry, you're just going through a rough time; the earth is a vale of tears, but when you leave it you will be received in the Lord's tabernacles.' But, no, that's not how it will happen, for they have done nothing to receive such a grace so easily and quickly.

Why does the church deceive people? It should say instead, 'You lazy individual, you'll have to sort this out by yourself! If your conditions are so bad, you must deserve them. But whatever your conditions, not only can you work on yourself every day, you can also help others.' But instead of this, they reassure them and say, 'That's how things are here, but on the other side you will live in splendour and abundance.' The reality is the other side will be the same, or even worse, if they haven't done any real spiritual work.

13 February

It is because the planets revolve around the sun that they receive light, warmth and life from it. If they were to cut the link they would die. And as everything in the universe is constructed from the same plan, man's organs and cells must remain linked to his spirit, his divine Self, in the same way the planets are linked to the sun, or they will deteriorate. Initiates have observed this truth, which is inscribed everywhere in nature, everywhere, except, unfortunately, in the human head.

People imagine that by cultivating anarchy and rebellion, by refusing to submit to the great cosmic laws, they are demonstrating their strength of character. But no, they are just showing their ignorance. For they become, on the contrary, increasingly dislocated and feeble. Humans acquire their true strength when they succeed in drawing all their instinctive impulses irresistibly towards their own solar centre. And once they have succeeded in doing this, harmony, plenitude and peace come to dwell in them.

14 February

Too often, we try to get rid of our problems by finding external solutions, when we should be trying to deal with them inwardly, so that we can shine all our inner light on them. We can compare this attitude with that of a mother who is obliged to discipline a disobedient child. Instead of first trying to understand the reasons for his behaviour (for there is certainly something to be understood), she gives him a couple of smacks, for the sake of a quiet life. But that is using the easy way out, and the child continues to disobey her.

Well, you must understand, our problems are also our children, in a way, and depending on how we deal with them we will manage to solve them, or we won't!

15 February

Both the Old Testament and the Cabbalah refer to God by different names. One of these names is the tetragrammaton *Iod He Vau He* יהוה. These four letters correspond to the four principles which, in the human being, are the spirit (*Iod*), the soul (*He*), the intellect (*Vau*) and the heart (the second *He*).

But for these four principles to manifest themselves and incarnate, a fifth principle is needed; this is the Shin ש, symbol of the union between spirit and matter, which is interposed between them at the centre יהשוה. These, then, are the letters in Jesus' name, which is Ieschouah in Hebrew. So, Jesus came to fulfil the mission symbolized by his name. Not only did he proclaim himself son of God, he also insisted that all human beings are the sons and daughters of God, and in the Lord's Prayer he asks them to work for the realization of the kingdom of God on earth: *'Your kingdom come, your will be done on earth as it is in heaven.'* Jesus taught humans that, by coming to incarnate on earth, they become the physical manifestation of the Deity, and he showed them the way.

16 February

You wait impatiently to see all your wishes come true, and there are so many things you wish for! This is natural, but, rather than wait for the day when you'll finally see your wishes realized, you should examine closely the nature of what you ask for. For the things you wish for will appear, but if you don't know what you're supposed to ask for in the first place you won't necessarily be happy when they do. Before wanting your prayers and wishes to be granted at all cost, ask yourself this question, 'Will the things I wish for produce something genuinely beneficial for myself and others?'

Before you ask for something, whatever it may be, you must be really sure that your desire conforms to the divine laws. If you are certain it does, continue to wish for it in the conviction it will come to pass.

17 February

If you wish to put the spiritual life into practice you must first refine the perceptions you have of your inner states, and it's normal for you to be unhappy with what you discover. But that's no reason to become discouraged and stop your work; you will gradually become stronger, and your sphere of activity will expand.

Those who remain seated in their armchair imagine themselves capable of the greatest exploits. It's only when they try to get up that their true strength becomes apparent, and that is when they are forced to lose their illusions. In their disappointment, they believe themselves weaker than they are, but in fact the opposite is true, for their strength begins with this new awareness. The difficulties they experience in detaching themselves from their past way of life are proof that they are trying to progress, to make efforts. And if they suffer, it is because they are finally beginning to feel and live and are moving towards a new world.

18 February

Our inner difficulties are analogous to a swamp. For as long as the swamp is not drained, we live in fog and are assailed by mosquitoes, because the swamp provides the best conditions for them to proliferate. Our life then becomes nothing but an endless struggle against fog and mosquitoes.

When you see certain people struggling for years with the same insoluble problems, displaying the same inner unrest and complaining about the same things every day, you would like to help them free themselves, but how? You talk to them, you explain to them that the external situation will not change, that it's up to them to change, but it's no good; they remain in their swamp with their mosquitoes. This happens to a greater or lesser degree, of course, but each one of us has swamps to drain and fill, so that the mosquitoes – our anxieties and suffering – can no longer live there.

19 February

Subject, verb and object: that is how a sentence is generally defined. The subject is the one that acts, the object is the one that is acted upon, and the verb indicating the action creates the link between the two. It is the verb that links, and without it nothing happens. In spiritual grammar, the subject is God, the source of life. The object is the human being, or the earth that receives life's juices. The verb is the angelic spirits that link the physical and spiritual worlds.

God, angels and humans: in other words, the divine world, the spiritual (intermediary) world and the physical world. So in spiritual grammar it is the angels that take the place of the verb: they are the intermediaries between the divine world and the human world. That is precisely why they are called 'angels', which means messengers.

20 February

It's not enough to desire and invoke good to come and live in you. As long as you do not eliminate certain impure, harmful elements, good will hover around you, but it will be unable to enter.

You may want, for example, to consecrate an object. You must begin by removing all the impure fluidic layers and particles left on it. It is always good to want to communicate with the forces of good, but you need to know that the first thing you must do on the physical plane is exorcise or free objects from all impurities, in order to then fill them with beneficial energies. Only then will you manage to impregnate objects with magic power.

21 February

We advance on the long road of life surrounded by all kinds of dangers, and we never know what might happen to us. But whatever the dangers, it is crucial we learn to master our fear.

Fear paralyses reflection; it causes the body to act in a wild and reckless fashion when faced with a real or imaginary danger. So if something frightens you, begin by remaining completely still for a few seconds, and take some deep breaths until you regain control of your heart, nervous system and limbs. If you allow your limbs to become agitated, you will lose all control over them, just as if you had opened the door of a cage containing wild animals: once they have escaped it is very difficult to get them to go back in. But if, instead, you replace this agitation with other responses, you will regain your inner peace, order will be restored and you will be able to act effectively.

22 February

Human beings walk the paths of life like empty vessels waiting to be filled. But why wait? Each person and each object they encounter has special qualities, and if they learned to recognize these they would no longer feel empty or alone.

Everything that exists in heaven and on earth can give you something good. But receiving it depends on you, for in order to receive you must be conscious and open up. If you go through life not only with your eyes and ears closed but, more importantly, with your heart and mind barricaded, you will, of course, remain in solitude and poverty. But open up, and you will realize that everything can serve as food for your inner life.

23 February

Do not allow yourself to be deceived by appearances: in reality, nothing is more effective than spiritual work. If it does not produce immediate results, it is because the world of the soul and spirit is more difficult for us to access than the physical world. But you must not become discouraged; if you allow yourself to be discouraged, it means you have neither science nor discernment. How long does it take to grow a lettuce? And how long for an oak tree? But how long will the lettuce last? And how long can an oak tree live? The same laws apply to our inner life: if you are content with just a lettuce, you will have it very quickly, but it will soon wilt. If you want an oak tree, however, you will have to wait a great deal longer, but it will live for centuries!

24 February

Do not be ambitious and subject yourself to rivalries, as this will drain your energies. Choose an activity where you have plenty of space, or perhaps are even alone, and then no one will prevent you from growing. If you go and plant yourself beside a great tree, it will complain you are encroaching on its territory. And what will happen if you venture into the territory of a wild animal? Be like a bird instead: it has a tiny little body, weak and light, and a tiny beak, but it is well equipped for the open air, for freedom. A bird has no ambition to obtrude on a wild animal; the only thing it asks for from the Creator is its song, joy and freedom of movement.

True sons and daughters of God are like birds; they do not want to establish their territory in the jungle. Every day they seek to fly away to the heights to bring back peace, light and joy, which they then share with all their brothers and sisters.

25 February

Truth is not an individual discovery, and humans can only claim they have found the truth once they have succeeded in living together in harmony. Yes, truth is not an abstract thing; it is the expression of a state of order in which everyone is in harmony and at peace with each other. Of course, to achieve this requires a great deal of adjusting, adapting and fine-tuning, and that is the work we all have to do.

You must understand, the only truth that exists is universal truth, and therefore truth only exists within unity. And how will this unity be manifested? When all humans feel they have the same fundamental needs, when they experience the hardship inflicted on others as their own suffering and the wrongs done to others as wrongs also done to themselves.

26 February

The day you realize you already have everything you need, you will discover how rich you are. Why don't you drill a few holes? You'll strike oil. Why don't you dig deep into your earth? You'll discover water there or precious stones. But you wait and do nothing; you are like beggars pestering passers-by: you are always bothering the Lord and his angels.

It is true, the most precious things that God has given us are hidden deep within us; we do not see them. Why not? Because he is a very wise father: if he spread all these riches out for human beings to see, they would make no effort; they would be content to simply take. And as they would not know the worth of these riches, what use would they make of them? Whereas, since they are forced to make great efforts to discover them, they will know how to appreciate them and use them in the cause of good.

27 February

Always place the highest ideal in your heart and soul. Even if it is unrealizable and inaccessible, cherish it all the same and give it nourishment. Life is wonderful, precisely because you have an inaccessible ideal. People quickly lose interest in things that are easily obtainable. Throw yourself into an endeavour that you know in advance will never be realized. For that is what will stimulate you, rekindle your enthusiasm and give poetry to your life. Psychology has not sufficiently studied this aspect of things. You will say, 'But it has nothing do to with psychology.' Oh yes it has; it is true psychology. So, do not ask yourself whether or not you are capable of achieving it; focus on the highest possible ideal: to make the divine life flow within you and around you.

28 February

In the exercise of their responsibilities – whether family, social, professional or political – it is very important for people to try and find a higher perspective inside themselves, one that will allow them to control all aspects of the problems they have to resolve. In that way, the decisions they make will be the fairest ones for everyone involved.

You will say, 'But you cannot be sure these decisions will be accepted. Most people are only interested in defending their own selfish interests, and it's not easy to persuade them to recognize the interests of others.' That's true, but even if some of your fine analysis and conclusions are not accepted, that's no reason to abandon your efforts. Once you have managed to raise yourself up to this higher point of view, there will be other occasions in life where you can make this viewpoint triumph. None of the efforts you make to advance along the path of lucidity and disinterestedness are ever wasted.

29 February

If someone has a fine physical appearance or good social position, that it obviously what others notice, especially on first acquaintance. But these advantages do not impress them for long unless they sense beyond the appearances something subtle and alive, for this corresponds to what everyone needs in the deepest part of themselves.

You already know this; you've already experienced it, but have you drawn the conclusion that, in order to encounter true love, you must work on yourself and create something pure, luminous, poetic and musical within? That is the only way to attract men or women to you who are also seeking purity, light, poetry and music. Never forget that what is essential is found in these subtle vibrations, these currents of energy that circulate between beings.

1 March

Spirituality does not consist in neglecting the physical body but in doing everything necessary to rid it of all the accumulated impurities that prevent it from manifesting the spirit.

What is the teaching of the Universal White Brotherhood? It is one that gives you the methods to do exactly that: to regenerate the physical body. In this way, all the most natural actions of everyday life, those that are indispensable to life itself, such as breathing, eating, drinking, washing, walking and sleeping, can become opportunities to do this work of regeneration. It's an entire science, unknown to most of those who call themselves spiritualists, which is why they experience so many complications and anomalies and can be so unbalanced. And not just them, for materialists also do not realize that the physical body, which they take such care of, was given to them to be made an instrument of the spirit.

2 March

As soon as you are presented with a difficulty or an ordeal, you must concentrate, reflect, pray and leave no stone unturned until you find the solution, the energies and, above all, the light that you need. Instead of complaining and allowing yourself to flounder, say to yourself, 'This is a good opportunity to start building something solid and unshakeable within myself'.

But don't wait until you are in real difficulty before making this sort of decision. Every day, with every little inconvenience, every little disappointment, every little blow to your self-esteem, you must be vigilant. Instead of saying to yourself, 'Why has such a thing happened to me? I don't deserve to be treated like this,' seize the opportunity to do some work. Don't lose this chance to build up your defences for the future.

3 March

Whatever our external conditions, we can always feel free in our inner world, the world of thought. But when we wish to express ourselves on the physical plane, we are dependent on conditions and are therefore limited. We must not be distressed if we do not obtain the results we hope for; we know that inside we have everything we need to live a life that is rich, beautiful and vast, a life that is useful to all creatures. Our thoughts and feelings reach far into space and allow us to come into contact with the entire universe, whereas our actions affect only a few people.

Even the most powerful being is limited in the realm of action. But if we improve our inner world, if we strengthen it with love and faith, we will also have more and more influence over the external world.

4 March

Those who abandon the Lord, who cut all links with him, allow the source of love within them to run dry. Then one day, faced with the successive failures of their emotional life, they ask themselves how it was they came to love all those men or women so much. At first they found them irresistible, and then over time they came to find them completely ordinary or even unbearable. Quite simply, the unique Being that inhabited a certain man or woman was no longer there for them. It was not the man or woman they loved but the Being who looked at them through his or her eyes, and they didn't know how to keep this Being with them. They behaved in a negligent, careless, selfish manner, and the Being who lived in this man or woman went away.

So, do not seek out men and women for themselves but in order to find in them the unique Being who, through them, will visit you.

5 March

It is important to understand the meaning of physical pain: it is a warning that we have wandered away from the right path. If we did not suffer we would go straight to our grave. Nothing is more dangerous than an illness that takes hold in the organism without giving the slightest alarm signal, for by the time the pain does arrive to warn us, the damage is often irreparable.

That is why, whenever you feel pain, rather than hurrying to relieve it with medicine you should ask yourself what caused it and look at how you may have been foolish or negligent. For if you do not heed these warnings, you will let the illness take hold within you, and it will become more and more difficult to overcome.

6 March

You can only interpret your present life correctly if you take a look at the past, for each event is the consequence of a previous event. You already know this, but you must also become aware of the opportunity you have to work on the present, which is the result of your past, so that all your good wishes and plans may be realized in the future.

In order to understand the meaning of a human life well, yours or anyone else's, you must see it as the consequence of a distant past but also, and more importantly, as the starting point for a new existence. Those who study an individual human life, without considering that it merely represents one link in a long chain, will inevitably make erroneous judgements.

7 March

Humans do not really see the riches of the world around them. Why not? Because they have a materialistic, and therefore superficial, view of it: they only look at how they can make use of scientific discoveries for their own satisfaction. And for precisely the same reasons, they are unaware of how they could make the most of their own body.

Our lungs, heart, ears, eyes, hands, liver, feet and so on are great riches, which most people do not know how to use. Driven by forces they are unable to control and which they are not even conscious of, they amble aimlessly here and there, swinging their arms and legs, listening to this, looking at that, chewing away at whatever they've put in their mouth. Materialistic philosophy has obscured their vision to such an extent they no longer have any notion of what true life is. It's time they understood how to make use of the resources of nature and of their own body in order to grow in spiritual stature.

8 March

True religion is the science of connection. So, it is no use repeating that the word 'religion' comes from the Latin *religare* 'to connect', if all Christians have in their heads is separation.

You will say, 'But the connection implied by the word 'religion' refers to our connection with God.' That's true, but, if a connection with God is accompanied by separation from everything else, what meaning does it have? The same bond that links the Creator to his creatures connects all creatures to each other and to all the elements of creation. True religion is based on an understanding of this link. So true religion also includes science, the knowledge of nature and its laws. That is why the separation between science and religion, of which some people are so proud, is totally meaningless. Those who separate religion and science have not truly understood either.

9 March

Kether: the crown; *Chokmah:* wisdom; *Binah:* intelligence; *Chesed:* mercy; *Geburah:* force; *Tiphareth:* beauty; *Netzach:* victory; *Hod:* glory; *Iesod:* the foundation; *Malkuth:* the kingdom. Learn to meditate on the ten sephiroth, the Tree of Life, with the consciousness that this cosmic Tree is also within you and that the only worthwhile activity is to make it grow, flower and bear fruit.

Don't worry about how long it will take before you are truly able to identify with this Tree of Life. Perhaps you will have to return to earth thousands of times to continue this work. But one day, these ten sephiroth, which dwell within you, will begin to vibrate, and the whole of your inner being will be illuminated by the lights of the Tree of Life.*

* See note and figure p. 373-375.

10 March

When I'm travelling and I arrive in a new town and see great crowds of people in the streets, I think of how these men and women each have their own life, their own history, their problems to resolve, their suffering and their loves, and of how there is a Being that sustains them all because it lives within them. If you also tried to have this thought from time to time, you would broaden your field of awareness; you would discover new regions where you would come into contact with higher entities.

Instead of troubling yourself with all sorts of useless or futile concerns, which do nothing but weaken you, concentrate on the universal Spirit, on the heavenly Father who created us, who carries and sustains us and lives in all his creatures. In this way, you will escape the burden of everyday existence, and you will feel the connection between your earthly self and your heavenly self begin to be restored.

11 March

Throughout the course of history, humans have become more and more successful at exploiting nature. Of course, nature is patient, but, when it feels that humans persist in upsetting the order that governs it, it retaliates, and this retaliation affects them not only in their immediate environment but also within themselves. They believe they are free to abuse nature in all manner of ways, with no fear of consequences. They cannot foresee that the very disorders they are creating in nature they are also creating in their own physical and psychic organism. And if they are incapable of getting on with each other, this is also because they don't respect the order that the Creator has established in nature and in their own being.

Those who have learnt to be in harmony with the order and will of the Creator do not exploit nature, nor do they exploit humans. They do not impose their will on others, and they do not attempt to win them over for their own personal advantage.

12 March

Everyone tries to get what's due to them by insisting on their rights. But they should leave all that to one side. Those who are always asserting their rights make a great deal of noise, and they often turn out to be as unjust as those they complain about, sometimes even more so.

You are following a spiritual teaching in order to learn the best way to 'settle your account'. You must understand that, in the future, the present codes of justice will no longer be current. The courts will no longer consider complaints lodged by those claiming their personal interests have been damaged but will respond to all requests made by those defending the common interest, the divine right. But while you are waiting for this day, be patient in the knowledge that, even though justice may be slow to arrive, it does exist, and one day it will show itself.

13 March

You believe you know what water and fire are, but you will only truly know them once you are capable of seeing them in their cosmic dimension as the two principles of creation. Their activity is symbolized by the cross. The horizontal line represents the movement of the feminine principle, water, which always tends to spread out and spill over the surface of the ground, taking up as much space as possible. The vertical line represents the activity of the masculine principle, fire, which, on the contrary, tends to concentrate its energies and soar towards the heights.

Water is therefore linked to the surface and fire to the heights. These two directions, the horizontal and the vertical, brought together in the figure of the cross, best represent the activity of the masculine and feminine principles within creation and all creatures. This symbol abounds in the universe.

14 March

People say, 'I'm sincere; I always say what I think, especially to my friends', and it's true: they destroy everything in their path. Sincerity is certainly a quality, but there's not much to be proud of in this kind of sincerity. Have they even asked themselves whether what they're thinking is right? No, and, besides, why would they? Hasn't humanity fought hard for the right to freedom of thought?

Granted, freedom of thought is a precious thing… providing we know what thought really is. What many people call 'thinking' is nothing but their mind's restless thoughts apropos of everything they like or dislike. But they're wrong. True thought is not linked to our likes or dislikes; it doesn't even originate on the mental plane, with the intellect, but on the causal plane.* It presupposes knowledge of the great cosmic laws. The first idea that enters your head is not a thought, and many of those who claim they say what they think should understand that, if they were truly capable of thought, they would keep quiet, or they would speak only after they had questioned the validity of their opinion.

* See note and diagram p. 376-377.

15 March

The Master Peter Deunov used to say, 'Should you cry when it's time to wash your shirt?... Should you cry when it's time to plant seeds in the soil?... Should you cry when it's time to grind the wheat?'

Washing your shirt, planting seeds in the soil and grinding wheat correspond to activities in the spiritual life. Which ones? Washing your shirt means to purify yourself. Planting seeds in the ground means to place good thoughts and feelings both in your own mind and heart and in the mind and heart of others. Grinding wheat means to prepare the bread of life. These three activities are accompanied by a certain amount of suffering – but suffering that's really beneficial! This divine suffering, when consciously borne, imbues everything we live, from then on, with beauty, perfume and flavour.

16 March

People sometimes wonder where the serene expression that characterizes the face of certain sages comes from. It comes, quite simply, from the fact that they've managed to overcome their fear of loss. They have risen to the summit of their being, where they feel something indestructible within, something that can never be taken away. Whatever happens, a true sage knows that the only reality, both for himself and for all other beings, is this summit, which is inaccessible to evil and shielded from all adversity: the spirit, the spark that God transmitted to all human creatures. But how can we reach that point? By working on ourselves, by purifying our thoughts and feelings so that we gradually dissolve the opaque layers which separate us from this spark and prevent us from sensing that it alone is real. Providence, as it is called by religion, comes from this deeply held conviction that certain beings possess, based on their experience that something within them is totally beyond reach and free from all vicissitude.

17 March

Whatever your circumstances, get into the habit of going deep within yourself, in order to find that quintessence called love, wisdom, gentleness, goodness, peace, inspiration, purity and gratitude. Simple objects you hold in your hand can help to bring out what is hidden in the depths of your being: a bird's feather, a leaf from a tree, a pebble… everything can become an intermediary, a means of getting in touch with your inner world.

And even a word written on a piece of paper can also suffice: you write a word, and thanks to this single word you enter your inner laboratory, and you find the 'flask' that carries the same name. The word you have written is like a reference, a detector; you hold it in one hand while you look for the flask in the other and, as there is an affinity between this word and a particular flask, you will eventually find it. I will never tire of repeating this: there are so many things at your disposal, but only so long as you make the effort to use them!

18 March

You build your true inner dwelling with wisdom and love. Wisdom's materials are solid, but they need to be supported by a living soul within if they are to last long; otherwise there will soon be mould on the walls. This living soul is love.

A house that's lived in doesn't deteriorate as quickly as an empty one. It is kept alive by the presence of people, their activity and their breath. It says to itself, 'I am someone's home, so I must stay standing.' But it will start falling to pieces if it's abandoned. So build your house with wisdom as the framework, but fill it with love to preserve it and make it solid. It will crumble if there is no love and no life circulating inside. And the proof is that once the soul leaves the body of a human being the body gradually decomposes. What was it that kept this building standing? The life that was flowing inside it.

19 March

Each religion has a particular day reserved especially for worship. For Christians it's Sunday, for Jews, Saturday, and for Muslims, Friday. But what real difference is there between these days? None. In the eyes of the Creator of heaven and earth all days are sacred; all days are divine. Good deeds can be done on Friday; good deeds can be done on Saturday and also on Sunday…

All days must be considered holy. Otherwise, there is no sense to any religion. Is there any point in calmly transgressing the laws six days of the week and then going to a church, mosque or synagogue on the seventh day in an attempt to make amends for the faults committed during the other six? It's grotesque! One day a week is not enough to progress on the path of wisdom, love and purity; a whole week is needed. Yes, every day, all day and all night, we must be present in God's church, because God's church is the whole of creation.

20 March

Water contains great mysteries, and some of these mysteries are linked to blood. Blood is sublimated water. Great analogies exist between water and blood, and not only between water and blood but also between water, blood and light. The sun's light, which is its blood, is also a form of water, a higher form of water. That is why, during the last supper that Jesus took with his disciples, he said, *'Those who eat my flesh and drink my blood have eternal life.'* This blood is the light that comes from the sun.

You think you know what water is, because it's part of your everyday life. But you don't; you are only aware of some aspects of it and some uses for it. But one day you will succeed in thinking of water as blood and light and really feel that it is. Only then will you really know it and be capable of using it in your spiritual work.

21 March

The cube's compact form has made it a symbol of stability, but also a figure of limitation, confinement and imprisonment. So, as it opens up and develops into a cross, there is a sort of liberation. Yes, that is why we must not see the cross just as an instrument of suffering and death; it is also a cosmic symbol that expresses all of life's possibilities.

Why, in the text of the Gospels, is Jesus' death followed by his resurrection? Because death is not the end; it is only a necessary step in the preparation for resurrection. Of course, I am speaking of resurrection in a symbolic, spiritual sense, not from a physical point of view. For resurrection to take place, there must first be death. Resurrection comes after death as a transformational process consisting of several successive phases. When understood in this way, it can be compared to a birth.

22 March

During winter, the archangel Gabriel concentrates energies in the seed. Conversely, the archangel Raphael liberates them during spring. And in order to liberate them, he first makes the seed die, so that everything contained within it can emerge to become roots, stem, branches, leaves, flowers and fruits... And from these fruits new seeds will come. Until this moment, the seed was an immobile creature – paralysed, sluggish – and could even have been so for thousands of years, waiting for the right conditions.

A seed appears dead, a bit like a corpse abandoned in a coffin. But in spring, when warmth returns, wherever there are seeds, there is resurrection: each one is like a half-opened tomb. The archangel Raphael begins his work, the stone is rolled away and the shoot appears. The cause of this resurrection is the warmth of the sun.

23 March

A seed that's been placed in the earth can be compared to a creature imprisoned in a tomb. When the angel of warmth comes, he wakes the creature, saying, 'Go on, get up now, come out of the tomb!' And then the life that was buried begins to stir: a little stem divides the seed in two, giving birth to a shoot that one day will become a magnificent tree. That is resurrection.

Before resurrection is possible, the tomb must be opened, and tombs are opened only by warmth. And warmth is love. Those who have a lot of love in their heart, spiritual, disinterested love, are able to open the tombs of their cells. As long as their cells are not animated and given life, they remain inactive, and people are unaware of all the riches they contain. But after resurrection, after this awakening of their cells, their consciousness expands, and they move in another dimension – the spiritual dimension – through everything they feel and everything they live.

24 March

What land was the Psalmist referring to when he said, '*I walk before the Lord in the land of the living*'? In reality, this land of the living is a state of consciousness, and in some way it is also our earth, or the etheric regions of our earth. For the earth is not only what we see of it; it is also a subtle world inhabited by luminous beings, angels and divinities.

Even Jesus can be found on this earth; he hasn't left it, since he said, '*I am with you always, to the end of the age.*' Of course, he has left the physical earth, but he still lives on an earth that is divine, luminous and alive, the etheric earth. And when the human beings that live here on our earth succeed in purifying themselves and reach a higher spiritual state, they also begin to inhabit this land of the living, and they come into contact with the great masters, with the angels and divinities and with the Christ.

25 March

Everything that exists is alive – to different degrees, of course – and life is characterized by the continuous emission of new radiations. Even the metal in your necklace, ring or watch vibrates differently from one day to the next. If you were really sensitive, you would feel a difference in the movement of the infinitesimal particles that the metallic matter is composed of. Why is this? It's because these objects are in contact with cosmic currents, and these are constantly being renewed. As you do not sense this, you believe there is no difference, but the reality is that not one thing anywhere remains the same.

And when the sun rises in the morning, it is also new. For there is a whole life in the sun: currents, emissions and eruptions… And if changes take place within the sun, how can these changes not have repercussions throughout the solar system on humans, animals, plants, rocks and even metals?

26 March

You would like to be loved, and you are unhappy because you notice people do not love you – or not enough! But try to understand that this attitude will make you even unhappier. How can you expect others to love someone who walks about with a long face, giving other people reproachful looks as though they were responsible for your unhappiness? Let's suppose it's true: no one loves you. I agree, it's certainly a great misfortune not to be loved. But the greatest unhappiness lies with you yourself being unable to love. Those with no love for others sign their own death warrant. So then, what prevents you, yourself, from loving? You are free. You cannot force others to love you; that's up to them, not you, but the decision to love depends only on you.

Try to make the first gesture towards others. Do not wait for others to always make the first move because you believe you deserve their love. Love, and you will be happy. And when they sense the happiness you get from loving, a happiness that manifests as light and warmth, you will see that others will also begin to love you.

27 March

There are always new things to learn, new efforts to be made; it's the only way to stay young and alive.

Today, in spite of the immense advances medicine has made, illnesses that were unknown in the past are appearing in prosperous, industrialized countries. Why? And why do so many people suffer from depression, anxiety and nervous disorders? Because, for most humans, even if they work, their ideal is to live a life of comfort, ease and pleasure. But nowhere in nature is there a blueprint in place for an easy life. Comfort, ease and the pursuit of pleasure introduce the germs of illness into humans and annihilate life itself: cells become lazy and no longer eliminate impurities; they allow themselves to become toxic, and the organism loses its capacity for resistance. Be wary of ease, comfort and pleasure; banish this ideal from your mind, for in reality it is the bearer of death.

28 March

Forests, mountains, rivers and seas… everything we see in nature is only its external cover, its physical body. We must try to go beyond that in order to discover nature's etheric body and the vibrations, emanations and currents that circulate through it.

But really, it's not enough to stop at nature's etheric body; you must go even further. And that is what disciples were taught in the ancient initiations: to 'lift the veil of Isis'. In the Egyptian religion, the goddess Isis is the spouse of the god Osiris. In this great female figure, initiates see a symbol of primordial Nature, from which issued all the beings and elements of creation. This Nature is impenetrable to the ordinary man or woman, but initiates have made her their main object of study. They want to know her, and that is why they make great efforts to understand the life forms she engenders and manifests herself through.

29 March

If you really need to be understood and appreciated by others, it is best to choose carefully the people whose respect you wish to gain. You will say, 'Oh, we know that,' but are you really sure? Are you certain that, in your desire to draw the approval and applause of the crowd, you never transgress the laws of goodness and justice?

When you participate in criticizing and ridiculing others, what are you doing? Deep down, you are well aware the criticism and ridicule are often exaggerated, but you have to put your oar in, just to please others, to make them laugh. And how many artists and even politicians make compromises for the sake of success! They're not bothered about whether they're appreciated by the wise; that's of no interest, there are so few of them! They would only have a very small audience or very few votes at elections. But is it really worth making compromises for this kind of success?

30 March

Alchemists say that, in order to make gold, you must start with at least one atom of gold, as a seed, for nothing in nature can be produced without a seed. The alchemical process is therefore similar to the growth or reproduction of a seed. A grain of wheat begins by producing one ear of wheat, and then one day there's a whole field! In the same way, for those who know the secret, a grain of gold can 'multiply' itself an infinite amount of times. We, too, possess this grain of gold, the divine seed given to us by the Creator. Now that he has given it to us, nothing and no one is able to take it away from us or make us lose it. But it's up to us to become aware that this seed exists, to awaken it and bring it to life, until it finally develops into a tree… a temple… the New Jerusalem… the Christ Child… So many images and symbols have been used to interpret this reality! All human beings possess this seed, and once they know where and how to look for it so they can work with it, the words 'life' and 'resurrection' will really mean something to them.

31 March

The capacity to embark on a divine, magnificent endeavour and follow it through unflinchingly is one of the rarest qualities. That is why a collectivity, or spiritual brotherhood, is necessary, even indispensable, for the proper evolution of human beings; it gives them the best conditions for persevering in their efforts. You are inspired by a book you've read and decide to improve your way of life, to do some exercises, but if you are alone you are bound to discontinue your efforts after a certain time, because you are not stimulated. However, if you are part of a collectivity, a spiritual brotherhood, you are influenced by its atmosphere and by other people's example. Then, even if you are tired, discouraged and feel like abandoning everything, you receive new impetus, and you continue your work.

1 April

Spiritual practice will not free you from all ills. It's better to be on the right path, but the fact that you are on the right path does not mean you have arrived at your destination. From one perspective, it is true that certain kinds of suffering will gradually disappear as you purify yourself and live in harmony with the world of light. But that does not mean the consequences of transgressions you have already committed in this life or previous lives will all be erased in one go.

Do not be surprised if certain types of suffering refuse to leave you, in spite of the new direction you have taken. To simplify things, we can say our good actions accumulate in one reservoir and our bad actions in another: we must be penalized for our bad actions, and we are rewarded for our good actions. So we experience events and psychic or physical states that are the distant or not so distant consequences of our past behaviour.

2 April

Salt is part of our daily meals. It is considered perfectly natural to place it on the table alongside water and bread. But how many stages the history of salt has passed through since it first appeared in that primordial ocean from which land gradually emerged! We cannot separate salt from our origins. It is vital to us. It not only gives flavour to our food, it also preserves it. But do you think about salt when you use it during cooking or at the table? You taste the food a little to see whether you have added enough, but it's your tongue that decides; your mind is elsewhere.

But don't you think it's time you deciphered this letter that God sends you through the intermediary of salt? What a long journey it's made, emerging from the sea and being dried by the sun, before reaching your home and table! And now that it's about to enter your body, you should study its symbolic meaning by meditating on Jesus' words: '*You are the salt of the earth.*'

3 April

Just as health is the result of harmony between the different parts of our physical organism, peace is the result of harmony between the different principles of our psychic organism: spirit, soul, intellect, heart and will. If it is so difficult to obtain peace, it is precisely because these principles are rarely in accord. A person may have wise, lucid thoughts, but if passionate feelings steal into his heart they will make him do foolish things. Or perhaps he is inspired by the best of desires but his will is paralysed. How can he find peace in the midst of all these contradictions?

You will never know what peace is, and you will have even less chance of achieving it, if you do not understand it as being a result, a consequence. Yes, peace is primarily a state of consciousness, one in which all the physical and psychic functions and activities of a human being are in perfect balance and harmony.

4 April

Instead of carrying a spirit of criticism or indifference with them wherever they go, disciples of an initiatic school try to understand everyone they meet: their needs, weaknesses and difficulties. And when they see how many people there are who are desperate and overburdened, who want to pick themselves up but can't, their hearts are overcome with love and compassion. They ask themselves, 'How can I help my brothers and sisters who are suffering and unhappy?' And that's when they become aware of all the treasures inside themselves that have accumulated over thousands of years and now, through neglect, are in danger of decay; they begin to draw on these treasures in order to give them away, and in doing so they realize how much richer they themselves have become.

5 April

In your day-to-day life, you will have noticed how often you lack patience! And it's this lack of patience that prevents you from expressing all your good qualities. Every day then, try to develop the ability to bear things more patiently. In other words, instead of immediately reacting to words and events, be quiet inside, breathe deeply, and call upon all the powers of peace, harmony and light to help you find a better attitude.

It is so important to work with breath! That is also why, when you do the breathing exercises in the morning, you can inwardly repeat the word 'patience' and be filled with its meaning, vibration and aura. And as you say this word, add an image that increases its power, until this virtue finally permeates your whole consciousness.

6 April

Some people believe the works of mystics or poets are nothing but fantasies. But no, these mystics and poets have simply entered another dimension of reality. We can call this other dimension a 'dream', so long as we don't confuse it with mere wanderings of the imagination or those adventures we experience during sleep. Initiatic Science considers dreams to be the seed of all reality. The material, physical world is only the crystallization of a dream, and even if the world disappeared the dream would remain because it alone is real: it is the dream that brings all sentient forms into existence. Every day, make a conscious effort to open the doors to this world of dreams. In it you will find all the essential elements you need to rebuild your life and give it meaning. And then even your face will reflect something of this world of light, beauty and unfailing joy. That is what true life is.

7 April

Human beings are naturally inclined to seek pleasure; everyone knows that, and it's normal. But is it wise for humans to trust their natural impulse when it constantly urges them to satisfy their instinctive needs? Should they yield to these urges without asking themselves where they will lead? Some people take pleasure in eating or drinking to excess, in offending others or taking what belongs to them and in destroying anything that upsets them. It's easy to understand why they find these things so pleasant, for nature offers such a wealth of possibilities! But this tendency to seek pleasure is not completely justified if it is not well orientated and controlled by wisdom and reason. The impulse itself is perhaps justified but not the actions it inspires, and it should not be given free rein to fulfil itself.

All needs are magnificent, motivating forces; there is nothing wrong with them in themselves: they only become harmful when the other factor, namely wisdom, isn't there to intervene and have its say.

8 April

True love is a manifestation of God himself, of his immensity and all-powerfulness. If you wish to attain this love, this force and vibration that commands matter, you must try to exchange only particles of light with the one you love. When two people feel a sublime love for one another, when they love each other for their soul and spirit, it takes only a look to fill them with wonder and ecstasy. Initiatic Science predicts that in the distant future, when a man and woman wish to bring a child into the world, they will simply be in one another's arms and will look at each other as though they were giving each other heaven. Their thoughts will be so concentrated, their love so intense, that a spirit will soon afterwards arrive to incarnate with them: its body will be made of the pure luminous particles given by its parents through their emanations alone. Of course, we are speaking of a far distant future. But such evolution is part of the plan of cosmic Intelligence.

9 April

When you eat with your family, with friends or even alone, are you careful to avoid making a noise with all the things you use? You're thinking, 'Why is he asking this?' Because it's important. If you watch your gestures while you're moving spoons, forks, knives, plates, dishes, glasses, bottles and so on, you will develop qualities of attention, precision and foresight, and these will stand you in good stead throughout your life.

So begin by practising self-control when you carry out simple activities like this, for otherwise you will continue to make mistakes all your life: you will bump into people or objects and say tactless things which will lose you a friendship or close doors to you. Use mealtimes to learn vigilance and mastery of your gestures: that is how you will awaken faculties within yourself that will enable you to deal with many difficult situations.

10 April

For those who have embraced the spiritual life, the greatest difficulty lies not so much in reaching a higher level of consciousness as in maintaining it. One day they win a victory over themselves, but the next day when the inner or outer conditions have changed they let themselves go a bit.

You ought to know, it's almost impossible to maintain permanence and stability on the spiritual heights. Stability is the culminating point of initiation, the moment when the disciple can finally say, like the hierophants of ancient Egypt, 'I am stable, son of stable, conceived and engendered in the territory of stability.' The territory of stability is the sephira Binah,* the region of the Twenty-four Elders. Even if stability is an inaccessible summit, link yourself to this sephira, and it will help you draw closer to it.

* See note and figure p. 373-375.

11 April

Why are human beings capable of the best and the worst? Because the nature of their consciousness places them between the lower and higher worlds. If they are not vigilant, if their consciousness is not awakened, dark forces begin to gain the upper hand. And conversely, when they link themselves to the forces of the higher world, they become a channel for powerful, beneficial currents.

Knowing this, each human being must understand how important their role in the universe is, for it depends on them whether the doors to heaven are opened or the doors to hell. Yes, since humans are at the boundary of the two worlds, it depends upon them, upon their attitude, whether it is good or evil that manifests on earth. In the same way that the sun is the doorway to divine forces in the solar system, human beings are the doorways to solar forces on earth. They therefore have an immense role to play in the universe.

12 April

Initiatic Science explains that the spirits of evil attack humans by enveloping them in thick fluids, like black clouds, but, if the point of a blade is directed at them, these fluids disintegrate and the dark entities retreat. It is said that Paracelsus possessed a sword which he used to repel the currents of hatred that pursued him. His science, his knowledge and also his character had attracted many enemies, who plotted his downfall. So, when he felt attacked in the invisible world by the dark forces projected onto him, he brandished his sword and wielded it in all directions.

But, of course, brandishing a weapon is not enough to rid yourself of dark entities. You must already possess this weapon within yourself: a well-trained will, directed by lucid, powerful thought and sustained by a feeling of disinterested love. Yes, physical weapons are not much help in spiritual life, and I do not advise you to use them. In order to win real victories, you must work with your mind, your heart and your will.

13 April

At the beginning of creation God said, *'Let there be light!'* and from this light he made universal matter. Every morning at sunrise, we have an opportunity to intensify this living light within us, thanks to the 'prana' contained in the air. Prana is an energy that exists throughout nature, in the earth, in water, air and fire, but it is mainly carried by the sun's rays, and through respiration we are able to capture it and introduce it into ourselves.

Each particle of this prana is like a drop of crystalline water, a tiny, suspended sphere, filled with light. While we are concentrating on the sun, we absorb some of these spheres, these subtle particles, through our breathing, and in this way we strengthen not only our physical body but also our psychic organism.

14 April

The journey we set out on, a very long time ago, will not end with our present life. This life is only one stage on the path along which all beings have had to travel since they left the bosom of the Eternal. And how many different regions they will have to visit before returning one day to the Source!

We must never forget we are only travellers on earth. But even amongst spiritualists, very few are capable of keeping constantly in mind the idea that they are travellers and must therefore never stop anywhere to put down roots. The road to be travelled is long, very long; if you are to continue in the right direction, you must continually observe, study and draw conclusions. And if you don't want to lose heart, you must keep your eyes fixed on the goal ahead.

15 April

Wisdom enlightens us; it allows us to distinguish between good and evil and so take the necessary steps to repel evil. But even our friends will not remain with us for long if we only ever call upon wisdom. Of course, wisdom attracts, because it shines and can be seen from far away, but it is cold, and people don't much like staying next to a cold light. That is why sages are often solitary beings, whereas those who are less wise but full of warmth are surrounded by friends. So what should we do? Is it better to neglect wisdom in order to avoid being alone? No, of course not, for those who allow themselves to be guided only by love risk being at the beck and call of others and end up being devoured.

Love binds and wisdom unbinds. That is why we must learn to harmonize the two currents within ourselves: to know when it is better to manifest love and when wisdom.

16 April

The Christ, the second face of God himself, has never taken a physical body; it only enters souls and spirits which are ready to receive it and become one with it. So Jesus, like all other great Masters of humanity and founders of religion, had a long road to travel before this spirit descended into him. If he was called Jesus Christ, it is not because he *was* the Christ but because he *received* the Christ. We can say that Jesus was God, but only in the sense that you and I, animals, trees, rocks and stars are also God. Since everything that exists comes from the divine substance, everything, in this sense, is God. The only difference is in the level of consciousness, and Jesus had the highest possible consciousness of God's presence within him. It is therefore this consciousness we must develop, until we melt into the Divinity and can finally say like Jesus: *'The Father and I are one.'*

17 April

Even though they have dedicated their life to searching for truth and have given the most evident proofs of their disinterestedness, their magnitude and their goodness, initiates and great masters are often considered to be people of very strange ideas. And yet ordinary people, those who are content to get by as best they can, are considered normal; they're the ones to take as examples! But what does the book of living nature say on this subject?

Here is one example, but there are many others: when the sun rises in the morning, which places on earth are first to receive its rays? The valleys or the mountain peaks? The mountain peaks, of course. So, the purest, noblest and most luminous beings are the first to discover truths. And, who knows how many centuries later, ordinary people will receive something of these truths.

18 April

The tree is, without doubt, the best image of the unity of creation: life circulates between its two extremities, from its roots, buried deep under the ground, to its branches reaching high into the sky.

But initiates have also expressed this unity by means of the symbol of a snake swallowing its tail. The head corresponds to the world of spirit and the tail to the world of matter. Spirit and matter are the two aspects of God manifest and active throughout all his creation. Nothing of what we see is separate from God: he represents the whole, and we are somewhere within him, like the cells of his immense body. And as we too are matter and spirit, we must try constantly to breathe into our own matter the life of the spirit, which is eternally renewed.

19 April

In reality, none of our possessions and none of the beings we are attached to belong to us indefinitely. We are constantly at risk of losing them, and when we do lose them we must call upon all those forces within us that are able to help us endure the loss. These forces are found in light, disinterested love, humility and sacrifice. So why not seek them immediately and consciously? It's difficult, when everything is going well, to convince humans they should concentrate on what is essential in order to prepare themselves for the ordeals to come. For they will come, that is certain; no one is spared. So do not wait for poverty, illness or misfortune to arrive before you seek spiritual direction. If you are already well armed, not only will you overcome them, you will also be strengthened by them.

20 April

When you meditate on holy images or sacred symbols, you attain a certain inner state that puts you in contact with entities of the invisible world. Magic, or natural magic as it's traditionally known, is based on the principle that relationships can be established between objects on the physical plane and beings of the spiritual world. This is where it differs from divine magic, theurgy, which works exclusively with names and numbers or, in other words, with principles.

Physical props are not necessary for contacting heavenly entities; initiates no longer need them. But it is a long apprenticeship. We begin by touching things, by tasting them; then we can breathe them, hear them and see them. Only at the end do we manage to feel and understand them. Feeling and understanding allow us to enter the spiritual world.

21 April

Faith and patience: if you nurture both within you in order to continue the work you have begun, you will succeed in materializing all your spiritual aspirations. Someone says, 'But for years I've wished for so many things that haven't come true!' That's because you don't know how to work, or because your wishes cannot be granted yet for certain reasons.

If your wishes concern collectivity, humanity as a whole, they are obviously a lot more difficult to realize than if they concern you alone. You wish for peace in the world, but so many other people want war, and so, of course, their wish prevents yours from being realized. That is why many more people and much more time and energy are necessary when you want to work for peace in the world and for the good of all humanity, for it is an enormous, long-term enterprise. But it's not unachievable. And it would be achieved if a large number of spiritual brotherhoods were created in the world, dedicated to this work.

22 April

Humans are so busy satisfying their physical and material needs that they no longer even sense the presence of another world within them; their soul and spirit have become foreign lands to them. Even if they've heard them mentioned, it means nothing to them, for the words have no meaning for them, and they wander like poor, misfortunate creatures through barren, sterile regions.

Those who wish to free themselves from this wretched situation must do everything they can to change the nature of their needs and seek the meaning of life in the subtle regions of the soul and spirit. Only when you have reached these regions will you finally live the true life. In one of his songs, the Master Peter Deunov speaks of a wondrous country where 'rivers flow, flowers blossom, fruits ripen, birds sing in celestial harmony and all people live as brothers and sisters'. You will say this wondrous country is inaccessible. No, it is found within the human soul.

23 April

The efforts you make on the spiritual plane are never wasted. Once you have succeeded in overcoming certain weaknesses and acquiring certain qualities, it is as though you have placed new stereotypes, new imprints, within yourself, and you will return in your next incarnation with these stereotypes, since they are permanent. The new physical body you enter will also be modelled and fashioned according to the degree of perfection you have reached, for the efforts you will have made to purify your subtle bodies will even produce changes in your physical body. It will become more resistant, more capable of receiving impulses from the spiritual world and of giving concrete expression to them through all your activities. The only work that bears fruit for all eternity is that of making the body a temple of the Lord.

24 April

We all know about the endless struggles smokers or alcoholics go through when they wish to give up their harmful habit. Why this conflict? Because our habits are bonds we create with our own cells, which are living beings. It is very difficult to break these bonds; our cells refuse to co-operate. It is exactly like wanting to divorce a man or woman who refuses to separate. Deciding to change is a heroic undertaking.

Tobacco, alcohol and drugs are examples everyone easily understands. But it's the same for all bad habits and inclinations. Faults and vices are entities endowed with their own will, just as illnesses are, and that is why they put up resistance.

25 April

Nothing in the world has greater significance than the encounter between the masculine and feminine principles. Neither men nor women can doubt that the two principles they represent are powerful agents or that they themselves influence one another in their desire to create. But what they don't know is what attitude to have, how to look on each other in a way that allows them to live in harmony, beauty and plenitude, instead of constantly provoking disorder, disillusionment and tragedy.

The entire universe is in motion thanks to the forces released by the masculine and feminine principles when they are in each other's presence. When properly orientated, these forces are capable of projecting luminous beams so powerful they are able to produce phenomena of cosmic importance.

26 April

Since we have come to the earth, we must submit to its laws and try to discover the best ways to express ourselves. No one can escape the earth's laws.

'What about very evolved beings, the initiates and great masters?' you will ask. They can't escape either. They arrive permeated with the fragrance of heaven, but the earth is a totally different world. Above, on the subtle planes, matter is obedient and malleable, subject to the slightest thoughts, the slightest desires. But the matter we live in here offers the greatest resistance. By making us come to earth, where we will always have difficulties to overcome, cosmic Intelligence has given our spirit the opportunity to flourish here in matter. For obstacles and ordeals are also forms of matter.

27 April

Once you begin to study a spiritual teaching seriously, to pray and to meditate, you see reality in a totally different light, for you gain a sense of perspective. Not only are you less obsessed with the weaknesses and limitations of others but you also begin to discover qualities in them you had never noticed before.

Paradise doesn't exist on earth; you will find imperfect humans and reasons to complain wherever you go, even in the best of places. Of course, if that is all you want to see, there will always be something to annoy you and make you suffer. Yes, but what makes human beings human is their capacity not to be dependent on conditions. Their inner life is a space they can constantly develop.

28 April

Wars are breaking out one after another in various places on the planet. And everyone laments the fact and asks why these wars exist. But it is simply because humans do not know how to take advantage of the good conditions peace offers them. It requires a great science to find the best ways for humans to occupy themselves during peacetime. But the truth is, humans are continually at war even during peacetime: they do nothing but confront each other in all realms of life. Politics, business, finance, religion and also family life are all areas of conflict, real battlefields. It's hardly surprising then if armed conflict is breaking out just about everywhere, bringing so much suffering in its wake! And then everyone begs the Lord to stop these wars and restore peace. But tell me, what has all this got to do with the Lord? It's human beings who should be asked to find the means within themselves to establish peace.

29 April

Spiritualists must not despise matter but must descend into it to give it life and organize it. And by 'matter' we should also mean the physical body. If we neglect it, under the pretext of devoting ourselves to the nobler functions of the mind and spirit, these functions will also eventually decline.

We mustn't leave our physical body in the same state as an abandoned house that ends up being used for shelter by insects and nocturnal birds. On the contrary, its owner must take the time to clean it, maintain it and give it life. When we descend into matter with this intention, it is never a fall. But we must know precisely how to distinguish between a descent and a fall. To descend into matter is one thing, to fall into it another. We must descend into matter with the aim of animating and enlightening it, so that we make our body the dwelling place of the living God.

30 April

In contrast to a tree, whose activity is periodic, the water of a river never stops flowing, even though it's not always the same water. The fact that there are exceptions, trees that never lose their leaves or rivers that dry up or overflow and change their course, is another matter; I'm taking the tree and river as general symbols of our inner states. Symbolically, the tree represents certain processes, and the river represents others.

Let's take the example of love. At some time in their life, all human beings get close to other human beings. That's what's called love, and thanks to this love they produce flowers and fruit. And then what happens? More often than not, they grow apart, they reject each other and become like bare, barren trees, which must wait for another springtime – another love – before they can become green once more and flower and bear fruit. But that is how ordinary people experience love. In evolved beings, such as initiates, the love that's expressed is like a river that never runs dry, and at this river all the creatures that live on its banks quench their thirst.

1 May

Why do so many remarkable people arouse terrible hostility? Because the dark forces they have expelled from their inner world return to attack them through other people who are disturbed by their qualities, virtues and force of character. By contrast, people who lead an ordinary life disturb no one, and everyone is happy with them.

But even though it's not easy to face external enemies, these are less dangerous than inner ones, and you have to use love, gentleness and patience with them. With inner enemies, on the other hand, you have to use firmness, authority and severity.

Unfortunately, humans more often than not do the opposite: they show patience and indulgence towards their inner enemies, and towards their outer enemies they are extremely severe. So is it surprising if they're forever struggling with problems from which they cannot free themselves?

2 May

The most useful thing a master does for his disciples is to draw their attention to their imperfections, for it is these imperfections that are the cause of their difficulties and suffering. All the while you do not know your weak points, you will be under attack and at the mercy of your enemies. To be able to defend yourself you must learn to recognize the enemy that's hidden there behind a fault, a bad habit or a wrong idea about things.

There is nothing worse than not knowing where your difficulties, suffering and misfortune come from, for you'll exhaust yourself firing cartridges into thin air. One day, you'll have no ammunition left, but your enemy will still be undefeated. So, at least try to understand that your Master is your best ally: not only does he teach you where your enemy is and how it manifests but he also gives you the means to react, and these means will enable you, sooner or later, to triumph.

3 May

How should we interpret Jesus' words: *'Ask, and it will be given to you'*? They assert the fact that praying, wishing and being insistent give us the power to effect certain changes, at least in our consciousness. We cannot perhaps change our outer circumstances, but when faced with them we can change our inner attitude to them, and we can alter our way of seeing and feeling so we no longer feel as afflicted and crushed by them.

Our greatest powers are not found on the physical plane but on the psychic plane. How many people with real reason to feel sorrow and despair have managed to find peace, light and freedom through prayer! And what about you? How many negative states of consciousness you could transform thanks to the ability God granted every creature to ask and pray!

4 May

It is not enough to find truth. Once you have found and understood it, you must remain true to it and work to serve it with tenacity, perseverance and patience. What is the good, otherwise? But how many people who claim to have found truth in a religion or spiritual movement no longer do anything or are content to preach to others! In reality, it requires endless work to find the truth, and we must unstintingly apply ourselves before we are able to live it in our everyday lives.

Unfortunately, you have to admit, constancy and stability are not the most common of human qualities. And yet, these are precisely the qualities demanded of disciples seeking initiation. In ancient Egypt, an initiate was considered to have won his greatest victory when he was finally able to say, 'I am stable, son of stable, conceived and engendered in the territory of stability.'

5 May

Even if you are not yet ready to live them, try to understand that there exist higher forms of love that you must aim for, if you really want your love to make you happy.

A woman cannot give everything to a man, nor a man to a woman, so they should say to each other, 'Please understand I am not able to bring you total fulfilment. Even if I gave you everything I possess, your heart is so immense, the entire universe would not be able to fill it, and your intelligence needs a light I do not possess. Only God can give you everything. So, consent to use me only as a means of getting closer to God. I will stay with you, but it will be God you are seeking through me.' That is how men and women should speak to each other, and then love would no longer leave them. It would become their permanent state of consciousness, and nothing would ever be able to trouble it. When you live love in this way, as a state of consciousness, you feel constant warmth inside yourself and a light that is never extinguished.

6 May

Like chemists, alchemists work with an element they call salt. But what they call salt and what they call mercury and sulphur have nothing in common with the chemical substances of the same name. Only the correspondences between them are the same: just as salt is the product of an acid and a base in chemistry, it is the product of sulphur and mercury in alchemy.

If we transpose these three elements to the psychic and spiritual planes, we have to understand sulphur to be the masculine principle, which manifests in us as spirit and mind, and mercury to be the feminine principle, which manifests as the soul and heart. And salt, the will, represents the balance that should ideally reign between the two. Will is expressed through actions, and it is through their actions that humans reveal the extent to which they have been able to create harmony between their mind and heart, their spirit and soul.

7 May

Imagine you wish to scale Mont Blanc, but you are not a mountaineer: you know you need a guide, for no one doubts a guide is useful, even essential, in such a situation! But when it comes to spiritual life, many people imagine they don't need a guide! Spiritual life is a much riskier undertaking than the ascent of a peak; there is much more danger of getting lost, of being crushed by avalanches or of falling off a precipice. And yet, people believe they need no one, they can get by on their own! It's extraordinary!

Nowadays, when spirituality, or what some people call spirituality, is in vogue, it's not surprising there are so many unbalanced, mentally disturbed people about. They tried to conquer summits without a true guide, and that could only ever end in a fall.

8 May

It is not enough for an activity to satisfy your desire for knowledge, bring you joy, or make you calmer and more relaxed. In every activity you must look for an opportunity to perfect yourself and become free inside. Yet even the manner in which humans practise art and science, as well as religion, betrays the fact that they are not really looking for a means of self-perfection. You will ask, 'But what does perfecting yourself mean, then? What must we do to succeed?' Perfecting yourself means to change the quality of your vibrations, so that you make them more intense or, in other words, more spiritual.

Everything lies in the intensity of your thoughts, feelings and the life within you; that is what initiatic Science reveals to us. Once human beings manage to live this intense life, all their activities, physical as well as spiritual, will only contribute to their evolution.

9 May

Of the four elements, fire is the most radical medium for transformation; nothing resists it. That is why initiatic tradition teaches that humans must pass through fire in order to be transformed – not physical fire, of course, but psychic fire. And on the psychic plane there is the fire of suffering and the fire of divine love. All those who have become so hardened that only ordeals can make them reflect and force them to alter their behaviour are obliged to pass through the fire of suffering.

In order to escape the fire of suffering, we must work with the fire of love, which will transform us, rendering us luminous and radiant; it will envelop us in its flames without burning us. And even if we still have to suffer, since we are still on earth, we will know how to pass through this suffering. The fire of suffering constrains and enslaves humans; the fire of divine love liberates them.

10 May

The number of the earth is 4, and that of Saturn is 8: 4 x 2. There is a very close relationship between the earth and Saturn, for the numbers 4 and 8 express the same reality on two different planes. The number 4 corresponds to earthly justice and the number 8 to divine Justice, the two sides of Libra. The number 4 is the square that encloses and imprisons, but also the cross with its four directions – north, south, east and west – that define the space within which we move. And the number 8, which is therefore a double cross, symbolizes cosmic balance.

The planet Saturn is under the influence of the sephira Binah,* where the Lords of Destiny reign, and when divine Justice needs earthly justice it sends beings to earth for the number 4 of earth to become their prison. So in order to escape from this prison, we must try to reach the higher manifestation of the number 8.

* See note and figure p. 373-375.

11 May

We sometimes feel that immensity is our soul's true homeland, and this feeling is not an illusion; it originates in our psychic structure. That is why those who refuse to take the needs of their soul into consideration will always feel a sort of dissatisfaction deep inside. Even if they have wealth, honour, success and glory, they will always sense something is lacking. And it's useless to try to deny or repress this feeling, for it exists to force us to walk along the path that will lead us to the source of light.

We are unable to see, hear, touch, explain or reach God. And yet we are filled with the irresistible need to set out in search of him. It is God himself who has placed this need within us, so that we never stop advancing. For that's what really matters: to never stop.

12 May

Those who have received the gift of a beautiful voice should know they possess a great treasure, thanks to which they can work wonders. But singers are often like spoilt children; they don't consider how valuable their talent is, and, most importantly, they don't reflect on the best way to use it. 'Which is what?' you will ask. To wrest humans from their mediocre, petty preoccupations, and inspire in them the wish to embrace a new life, dedicated to beauty and light. And then the names of these singers will be recorded in the book of life. It will be noted: they have opened hearts, enlightened minds and saved souls from tribulation and death.

All activity born of a disinterested idea and placed in the service of a divine cause possesses the seed of immortality. Those who are conscious of this law acquire true wealth, for winning a soul to the light is higher than anything else.

13 May

Nature is alive and intelligent. And yet most humans treat it as though it were dead and stupid, and that is why life no longer vibrates so intensely and powerfully within them: little by little they paralyse all the faculties of knowing, understanding and feeling that God has given them.

If you do not consider stones, plants, water, air or the sun to be alive, why would you try to communicate with them? With this attitude, you blunt your faculties of perception, and when you do that you limit yourself. Whereas, if you believe nature is alive and intelligent, you will make the effort to understand its language and discover ways to communicate with it within yourself.

14 May

One day, everyone will become exactly as God envisaged and meant them to be, as they already are in their higher Self. It is this certainty that must give meaning to everything we presently experience. In spite of how difficult it is, nothing must stop our progress along the path that leads us to the light.

Watch the sun rise; allow yourself to be absorbed by this life, by this radiance. Begin the search for your true Self in this outpouring of light, in the radiance that is the expression of divine splendour. The day you discover it, the day you learn to identify with it, you will realize that you have never ceased to live in its power, love and light, and that, through your life and activities, you are able to participate in the gigantic work that's taking place throughout the universe.

15 May

Don't be under any illusions; you will not find a single perfect creature on earth. Whether they show it or hide it, everyone has at least one weakness, even several. Even initiates have at least one weakness: vanity, pride, greed or sensuality… But the reason that initiates are more advanced is that, firstly, they are conscious of their weaknesses and, secondly, they try to overcome them through all possible means.

Inasmuch as they have incarnated on earth, all beings, however elevated their spirit, receive a heredity that is more or less defective, and this is what they must work on. Initiates achieve this, thanks to their other qualities and virtues. And when they have succeeded, they become even greater, because they have been able to transform a raw, crude matter into a more refined matter, which they can then use for their work. Initiates demonstrate the extent to which the power of the spirit is able to master everything. Most humans, however, are plagued all their life by faults they cannot correct.

16 May

The Master Peter Deunov used to say, 'Place goodness as the foundation of your life, justice as its measure, wisdom as its boundary, love as its delight and truth as its light.' Goodness, justice, love, wisdom and truth are five necessary virtues for the harmonious development of man. True science lies in the knowledge of the links these virtues maintain not only with our physical body but also with our psychic and spiritual bodies. Goodness is linked to the legs, justice to the hands, love to the mouth, wisdom to the ears and truth to the eyes. And truth belongs to the spirit, love to the soul, wisdom to the mind, goodness to the heart and justice to the will.

17 May

'Seek first his kingdom and his righteousness, and all these things shall be yours as well.' The kingdom of God represents the highest ideal to which a human being can aspire. When you place yourself in the service of this ideal, you attract all blessings.

Everything you may wish for, apart from the kingdom of God and his justice, in other words, apart from light, love, generosity and brotherhood, can only weigh you down, make you poorer and make your life more and more difficult. Perhaps after tasting certain pleasures or achieving personal success you will feel satisfied for a few moments, but you will soon tire of it, and you may even have to pay dearly for that moment of satisfaction. That is why these words of Jesus: *'Seek first his kingdom and his righteousness, and all these things shall be yours as well'* are said to be the absolute quintessence of initiatic Science.

18 May

So many believers imagine heaven exists in order to give them health and success! And if they encounter illness or failure, it's obviously the devil that's sent it. Well, no, it could also be heaven, concerned about their development. For heaven doesn't really take their suffering into consideration; it only wants them to improve. They can shout, cry, sob and threaten as much as they like, that doesn't bother heaven, for it only asks that they become more intelligent, wise and enlightened. And unfortunately, it is only after they have been shaken up and given some nasty shocks that this result will be achieved.

The noise of wars resounds all over the earth, and many people ask why heaven doesn't intervene to put an end to it. The reason is that heaven cannot forcibly control human hearts and minds and make people understand the advantages of peace. They are free. It must leave them to suffer so they can reach this conclusion themselves. And this is also true for many other events in their life.

19 May

Everything on earth is transient, ephemeral, but above our heads the sun remains, unchanging and eternal, and that is where we must direct our gaze. When you seek the truth you must turn to something that doesn't pass away, that doesn't change. But it seems difficult for humans to find the right attitude towards the sun: either they neglect it or they exaggerate its role; either they think it has nothing to do with religion or they worship it as an idol. They are mistaken in both cases. By giving the sun no place in their inner life, they are depriving themselves of an essential element. But to focus on the physical sun as though it were an idol is to regress to the mentality of those primitive peoples who worshipped the forces of nature.

The sun must simply be a way of finding God, our inner sun. Each day, by contemplating it, by exposing ourselves to its rays and identifying with it, we increase our divine light, warmth and life.

20 May

From 21 April to 20 May, the sun is found in the sign of Taurus, where the moon is exalted, and where Venus, the planet of regeneration, has its home. Taurus is the sign of fertility and abundance. That is why it is important to work with the forces of nature during the full moon of May to attract heaven's blessings for the harvest and livestock but also for human beings.

For, if humans know how to receive the influences projected throughout the cosmos during this period, they too can benefit from them on the physical and spiritual planes. That is why, through their songs, prayers, meditations and invocations of magic, initiates work to create lines of force in space which attract heavenly currents. And then they project these currents onto those who are vigilant, awakened and capable of participating in all the events unfolding in heaven and on earth.

21 May

Instead of giving free rein to your lower nature by constantly challenging others and arguing with them over everything and nothing, try learning to argue with all the dark entities that live inside you. These entities, which have been plaguing you for many incarnations, have finally become embedded in you in the form of bad habits, and you must persuade them to keep quiet. At the same time, call upon your higher nature, which manifests through all the wise and enlightened entities also living within you. Let them speak, and accept their good suggestions, for these will be useful to you and to others.

How many people say they want to be useful to others! But good feelings and intentions are not enough. Those who wish to help others must become conductors of divine life, and for that they must rid themselves of everything that may attract dark forces.

22 May

The reason humans commit so many errors of judgement, make so many mistakes and experience so much suffering is that they don't know what they have come to earth to do. They come, and then they go. Where do they come from, and where do they go back to? They don't know. But there is only one answer to both these questions: God.

We have left God, and one day we will return to God. Which paths will we take, during the course of our many incarnations, before we return to the Source? That depends on us. God has planned an extraordinary destiny for humans. We occasionally receive a fleeting glimpse of it, and we must cling to these visions with all our might. Everything that happens to us on our return path represents stages of the journey. These stages must never erase from our memory the vision of what we will finally become when we return to the bosom of the Eternal, with all our experiences and all the qualities and virtues acquired and developed along the way.

23 May

Cosmic Intelligence hasn't sent us to earth for us to think only of leaving it once we've arrived, under the pretext that heaven is our true homeland. The desire to abandon earth for heaven is just as harmful to our physical and psychological health as the desire to abandon heaven for earth.

Some people, once they have decided to pray and meditate, run the risk of giving way to laziness or even mental confusion, for they come to the point where they can no longer distinguish between what's real and what's imaginary. That should be avoided at all costs. Even moments of ecstasy, which are the most desirable states for a mystic, are very detrimental to health if they are not experienced in moderation, with caution and wisdom. It is said that God is a devouring fire, and the physical body is not built to endure this fire for any length of time.

24 May

Freedom is not found on the physical plane. Freedom is found on the atmic plane, which is the world of the spirit. So in order to be free we must identify with our spirit. The more we achieve this identification, the more we strengthen ourselves and escape the conditions around us.

Figuratively speaking, we could say identifying with the spirit is like climbing above the clouds. Those who stay below the clouds are always dependent: they must wait until the clouds decide to clear before they can see the sun, and while they're waiting they're exposed to darkness, cold, fog and rain. As they don't realize they're responsible for this situation themselves, they complain, 'The sun is hidden'. But the sun is not hidden; they themselves have allowed clouds, in the form of their dark thoughts and feelings, to come between the sun and their soul. They only need to disperse these clouds or project themselves above them and they will immediately have light, and what freedom they will feel once they have light!

25 May

Why is it so important to form spiritual communities? I will give you an image: engineers build immense power stations capable of supplying energy to entire regions. Well, a spiritual group can be compared to a power station: it is able to provide the energy needed to project light far into space. For human minds are veritable batteries. They simply need to be united and put in contact with a divine idea; the currents they project will be received by vast numbers of other minds in the world, and these people will also decide to work for a divine idea.

You pray, meditate and sing together, but you are not yet aware of the immense possibilities these activities offer for the good of all humanity. It is time to become conscious of it and do this work, so that the light of the kingdom of God can be received by the greatest possible number of minds on earth.

Love the Creator, the One who is the origin of all life, and you will feel him manifesting in every creature. It is he, the One, whom you will love in others, and only he can fulfil the longings of your heart and soul. So many men and women, famous throughout history for their amorous adventures and conquests, have had tragic destinies precisely because they did not understand this truth.

The beings of flesh and blood you claim to love or to be looking for are only intermediaries, conductors meant to transmit divine energies. If you wish to continue to love them, think of restoring contact every day with the world above. You don't need to worry about who you will love or who you wish to be loved by. First love God and he will appear to you; he will smile at you and fill you with joy through his creatures. You will love them and be loved by them, because it will be the Deity dwelling within them that you will love, and they will also discover him through you.

27 May

Imagine a young musician playing a new piece from sight. If he doesn't pay great attention, he will make a few mistakes, and once these have been made they will be imprinted in him as stereotypes: if he is not very careful he will make the same mistakes in the same places even twenty or thirty years later, even when he knows the piece by heart, and it will take a great deal of time and effort to correct them! That is why, when a musician is sight-reading a new piece, he must take all the time he needs to create perfect stereotypes. One day he will even be able to eat and sleep while he plays and not make a single mistake, because everything will be imprinted perfectly in his subconscious.

What is true for music is equally true for many other activities in life. When you begin with great care and wisdom you avoid making mistakes, and you therefore save time, energy and effort.

28 May

Human relationships are very complicated things, whether they are with members of your family, friends, colleagues from work and so on, or even with people you don't know. If you wish to maintain harmony and mutual understanding, you must forget yourself a little; try not to always put forward your own points of view and tastes, but demonstrate understanding, tolerance and patience. It is a sacrifice, but sacrifice is a force; yes, this is the great idea you must bow to. Of course, there's something in you that resists: sacrifice implies limitation and loss. But you must understand it's your lower nature that retaliates, whereas your higher nature rejoices.

Stop bringing everything back to yourself, to your opinions, your feelings and desires. Concentrate on a noble, luminous ideal, for this will swallow up the thousand difficulties you encounter every day in your relationships with others. You will no longer even see these difficulties, and even if you do they will no longer affect you.

29 May

When Jesus said, *'I am the light of the world'*, he was identifying with the sun. Who *is* the light of the world, in effect, if it isn't the sun? The sun is the visible, dazzling image of the Divinity. When you identify with light it means you recognize you are not just your physical appearance but you possess another nature. You know you are made of a spiritual quintessence, and you decide to let it take your place.

For Jesus to have been able to say, *'I am the light of the world'* and to have found this light within himself and risen to its level, he must have succeeded in identifying with the spiritual sun: the Christ. And that is true love, the irresistible force which impels humans to seek what is most pure and most divine within themselves and, once they have found it, to become one with its reality. Yes, love is attraction; it arises from the spark God has placed within the soul of human beings, because of which they experience the need to find him again and become one with him.

30 May

If you have the necessary qualities, you can perhaps impose your will on humans, to show them how powerful you are. Before the Lord, however, you must do the opposite and become self-effacing to the point of merging with him and becoming one with him. Yes, when you allow yourself to become small before the Lord's greatness, even to the extent of disappearing, you in fact become great, whereas if you assert your own will over his you only weaken yourself, and you become nothing.

And what is it within you that must diminish itself before the Lord? Your lower nature. As an element that's separate from the Whole, it must die, so that, through your higher nature, you can participate in the limitless life of the Whole. And then it is no longer you that live but the Lord that lives within you. Of course, we must understand this as a psychic, spiritual process. The goal of all spiritual discipline is for the disciple to finally recognize that he or she is God himself; that is the meaning of the Jnana Yoga saying: 'I am He'.

31 May

There are role models and there are role models. Some people get themselves noticed because they stand out or are successful in a certain area, and then lots of other people immediately want to imitate them. But if their superiority derives from their money, possessions or social standing, they are not good role models. Why not? Because they will be leading people along a path where they are constantly driven to dominate others, to undermine or humiliate them. Whereas those who are characterized by their spiritual qualities of kindness, wisdom, self-control, nobility, generosity, purity and selflessness are good role models, for they help others walk along the right path and find true happiness.

All humans need role models, not models of material and social success but ones that make them aware of their true wealth, the riches of their heart, soul and spirit.

1 June

While continuing to carry out the tasks and responsibilities imposed on them by their family, their material conditions and society, spiritualists try to become consciously aware of the reality of those distant worlds that constantly send us messages.

Brooding over problems isn't the best way to resolve them. On the contrary, it is better to forget them for a while and learn to make use of the spiritual centres God has placed within us to communicate with the higher regions and their inhabitants, to bring ourselves into harmony with them and enter into their aura, their happiness and peace. Once you have succeeded in capturing even a few of these waves, you will hear all these celestial entities speaking to you about your future, about the riches you possess and the life that will be yours once your consciousness has finally awakened to the divine world.

2 June

Water is naturally purified by infiltration or evaporation. As it infiltrates the earth, it passes through different layers where it deposits the impurities it has collected on its way and re-emerges purified and drinkable. From a symbolic point of view, this is the path that most people take: they are constantly being constricted and crushed by events, and it is this suffering, this intense pressure, that purifies them.

Spiritualists try to choose the second method: evaporation. They are purified by the sun, not by the earth. Just as water evaporates under the effect of the sun's rays, those who expose themselves to the spiritual sun are warmed and rise into the air, symbolically speaking. This is how they purify themselves, and during this purification they experience great joy. They then return to earth in order to 'water' plants, animals and humans.

3 June

Form is always closely connected to matter, and those who only concentrate on form lose the intensity and subtlety of their life and become rigid. But the law of life is evolution: new currents and new forces are constantly appearing in order to break those fossilized forms.

Take stones, for example: there are always hammers and machines coming to break them up and grind them to pieces. It is the destiny of stones to be broken up. And all humans who allow themselves to be controlled by matter have the same destiny. One day, they will also be broken up. You could say that life oscillates between two poles: spirit and matter. And when the spirit, which is characterized by mobility, flexibility and subtlety, comes to manifest itself, nothing can resist these forces of renewal. All forms that have become old and rigid will disintegrate. Time, in other words the forces of life, will always overturn them eventually, in order to force them to renew themselves.

4 June

The problem of social inequality will never be understood correctly or resolved until humans accept that their conditions in this incarnation depend on the way they lived in their past incarnations. Workers who are exploited by unscrupulous bosses protest indignantly. 'Why this injustice?' they ask. And the bosses themselves, who consider it normal to live a life of ease, of luxury even, do everything they can to preserve their privileges. But what neither the bosses nor the workers know is that a worker who suffers and protests has, in many cases, been a cruel, unjust boss in the past, which is why in this incarnation they have been placed in conditions where they must understand how they made their former subordinates suffer.

So now, every boss and company director must say to themselves: 'I am fortunate enough to be rich and powerful in this life, but if I treat my workers and employees unjustly I will suffer the consequences in a future life. Lord, help me to make them happier.' And there's nothing to prevent employees from praying for their boss to become more enlightened: perhaps they would derive some benefit from doing so.

Magic is the science and practice of influences. If an object or being exerts a beneficial influence on the surrounding environment, we say it is white magic, and if the effect is disturbing, disruptive or destructive we say it is black magic. In this sense, everything can be considered magic: gestures, words, looks, sounds, colours, geometric shapes… By the same token, animals, plants and minerals also possess a magic power, in so far as they exert an influence over people and either attract or repulse them and heal them or make them ill. When we look at the sun, the stars, mountains and lakes we sense the effect and influence they have over us, and in our own way we also influence them.

Everything in the universe is magic, because all things are constantly influenced by one another. Once you have understood this, and you try hard to think, feel and act in a constructive and harmonious manner, you will become a white magician.

6 June

Science, like religion, is responsible for the evolution of humanity. The true scientists are those who see the possible consequences of their discoveries in all realms of life, including the psychic realm; for the physical and psychic worlds obey the same laws, and every discovery made in the physical world can also be applied to the psychic world.

Physicists have made discoveries about the waves and energy currents that circulate throughout space, as well as about light and its power. The practical application of these discoveries has been extraordinary, of course: the telephone, radio, television, the laser… and so many more besides! But what benefits have human beings themselves derived from these for their own evolution? They should have understood that they themselves emit and receive waves and currents, that their thoughts possess the same powers as light. It is dangerous when the only applications for scientific progress are practical ones that make life easier. Scientific progress should indicate new psychic and spiritual directions. Only then is it true progress.

7 June

Examine the way you walk so you can improve it if necessary. Try to walk with suppleness and lightness, with your head up. It's a very bad habit to walk stooped, as it is to hit your heel hard against the ground with each step: people who walk like this don't realize they are doing violence to their brain, for each jolt has repercussions inside on their entire nervous system, and after a few years they will think and act in a coarse and violent manner.

If you are tired after half an hour or an hour's walking, this also means you do not know how to walk. Walking gives you energy if you know how to adopt the right rhythm, and even if you were tired at the outset you will gradually feel your strength return. There is a rhythm for walking which isn't tiring, and everyone should try to acquire it. When you feel forces beginning to circulate within you as you walk, it means you have found the right rhythm.

8 June

Everyone is spontaneously attracted by certain people, because they find them nice, pleasant, amusing, original or seductive, or sometimes they don't even know why, and it has nothing to do with any moral value the person may possess. This is natural, but as friendship and love imply trust, why not try to get better acquainted with the people you wish to make friends with?

In general, everyone possesses different qualities and virtues, which they manifest to a greater or lesser extent, depending on circumstances. But there are other qualities they are sure to manifest whatever the circumstances. Try to discover what these are so you know what you can count on. As for their faults, these don't stop you feeling affection for them, but you must also be aware of them, so as not to expose yourself to disappointments and misunderstandings.

A religion is only true in so far as it resembles the solar religion. And the religion that Jesus brought *was* a solar religion, whatever Christians may say; they have not yet understood his teaching correctly. Yes, when Jesus says, for example, *'Be perfect… as your heavenly Father is perfect'*, how can we have any idea what divine perfection is like? Only by taking the sun as a model.

In order to become truly perfect, we should not even take saints or initiates as models, only the sun. Of course, initiates will give you the example of great virtues, but they know they are nothing compared to the sun. That is why they express themselves with humility; they defer to the sun as their example, for they know that whatever they may do, their light, warmth and life cannot compare to the light, warmth and life of the sun.

10 June

How many different thoughts and feelings human beings can have during the course of a single day! That is why their vibrations and emanations never remain the same. But these changes are usually imperceptible, and it takes many years before others notice that their face, the colour of their skin, their figure or the very substance of their body have altered.

Those who abandon themselves to a chaotic life, who nurture crude thoughts and feelings, are degrading their entire being, and soon their expression, their look, their voice and gestures will show the effects of this degradation. But if they really try to attune themselves to the divine world, to respect its laws, something within will gradually right itself and become clear and pure. Just as the water of an underground stream transforms the rocks and pebbles it flows over, so the divine currents that pass through human beings impregnate the particles of their body with light, and then a true metamorphosis begins to take place within them.

11 June

News of a tragic event or a happy surprise can provoke overwhelming emotion in a person. Yet, what is news? How can something immaterial upset people to such an extent it makes them ill or go mad, even kills them… or, on the contrary, produces a miraculous healing?

Take the case of a mother who has been paralysed for years. One night a fire breaks out in her house. Her child is sleeping in another bedroom. The thought that her child could be burnt alive is such an intense shock to her that she jumps out of bed to grab him and carry him to safety. Yes, the contact between her nervous system and her muscles is restored once more through the force of her love. Of course, this happens only rarely, but it does happen. So why not study these phenomena? You'll say you've known about such things for a long time. Yes, perhaps, but has that ever led you to study these processes in order to improve some of your inner states?

12 June

It is absolutely impossible to interpret sacred books correctly without a discipline based on the development of our spiritual organs. When we develop these organs we acquire the ability to project ourselves into the higher worlds to investigate them. From below, we can see only separate parts of reality. And if we are unable to perceive an order and structure, in other words the links that unite all the elements and stages of creation, we cannot correctly interpret texts that were inspired by a vision of divine unity.

The sacred books of humanity are the interpretation of experiences that certain beings have had in the world above, a world different from the one we perceive with our five senses. So, in order to understand these beings, to understand their thoughts, we must go seeking on high, as they did, to see what they saw and feel what they felt.

13 June

When heaven offers a great mission to an initiate who is reincarnating on earth, it doesn't hide all the ordeals he will have to go through, for by triumphing over these ordeals he will succeed in fulfilling his mission. Of course, he's not overjoyed to see what will happen to him, but it's the end that counts, nothing else, and so he accepts. But the Lords of Destiny take away the memory as soon as he incarnates: he no longer knows anything about his mission or the ordeals he must go through. He's like an ordinary man, and he suffers, until he understands that heaven has used him to realize its great plans and that if his life had been easy he would have done nothing, would barely have caused a ripple, like many others.

Of course, not everyone can explain their ordeals by saying they've been entrusted with a great mission by heaven, but they should know that, depending on the way they overcome their difficulties, heaven will judge whether or not they can be counted on in the future.

14 June

Why do you always comment on others' imperfections? Try, rather, to perfect yourself. When your parents and friends see how much you have changed they will be forced to change themselves. The work you do on yourself is contagious; it's like magic: others sense it, and they are encouraged, sometimes even in spite of themselves, to try and improve. It's not easy to change humans. The Lord himself hasn't succeeded yet, so how can you expect to?

Leave other people alone, then, and just think about working on yourself. Perhaps, once they sense you have become wiser, stronger, more generous and more brotherly, they will be encouraged to imitate you. Don't waste your time criticizing and complaining. Just deal with yourself. You will have far fewer worries if you do; you will no longer torment yourself, and the efforts you make in this way will accelerate your evolution.

15 June

With the technical means now at their disposal, chemists are able to extract a great many elements from metals, minerals and plants which are then used in the manufacture of different products. And they will continue to penetrate more and more of nature's secret treasures. They will discover that everything in existence is composed of elements endowed with particular properties that can benefit human beings.

And don't be surprised if I say that human beings are also 'nature'. When you make the decision to enter the immense laboratory of your own being, you will find all the elements you need for your physical, psychic and spiritual development. There is nothing to prevent you from searching for these elements outside yourself, but never forget everything is inside you. You must make every effort to become conscious of and develop your inner wealth and power. Once you truly feel you carry all these elements within yourself, you will possess a treasure trove inside, which you will constantly be able to draw on.

16 June

Whatever scientific and technological discoveries are made, we shouldn't count on them to find solutions to the problems facing humanity. And even the most exceptional researchers will fail to find the meaning of their life if they are content to explore matter. Why? Because the scope of their research remains outside themselves, like their apparatus, their laboratories and the subjects they study.

That is why you'll see scientists who've made fantastic discoveries and even received the Nobel Prize lose all sense of inner direction. If they had known the philosophy of the initiates and applied their methods, they would also have received inner strength and enlightenment from their discoveries. It's such a pity they didn't! What sense is there in making discoveries that make life easy for others, if you remain plunged in darkness and disarray yourself?

17 June

So, you haven't been able to find your place in society? And you can't find the conditions you need to make your mark with the talents and abilities you have? That's no reason to feel inferior or useless. When you participate in the work for the coming of the kingdom of God and his justice on earth, your worth increases in an extraordinary, unique way. When the idea of the kingdom of God is present in each of your thoughts, feelings and actions, you feel something develop within you which gives you your true place, and nothing and no one can take it away from you.

And what does it matter if others occupy centre stage! They'll have to leave it one day, anyway. And during this time, while you are secretly working for the kingdom of God, you feel something growing in your soul which no human esteem and no human glory can eclipse or even equal.

18 June

We must learn from the sun for it is the image of perfection. You will say, 'But what can this ball of fire teach us? The sun doesn't think; it doesn't speak!' Ah well, that's where you're wrong. Its light, warmth and life are a language, one of the most eloquent. Just think of this: it sends its light and warmth into the universe without bothering to know whether those who benefit from its rays are either deserving or grateful. Isn't that a language? It gives them all light, warmth and life, without exception.

The sun always presents you with the image of a radiant, generous being, and when you look at it you feel its influence. Even if we assume it's not an intelligent, rational creature in the sense we understand it, the contact we have with its warmth and light can only inspire us with more fraternal feelings towards others: more patience, leniency and forgiveness.

19 June

Your personal life is of little significance, so why make it the centre of your concerns? What are your little problems compared with the immensity and abundance of the life a spiritual teaching provides? If you're forever focusing on yourself, on what you like or dislike, on what does or doesn't suit you about other people, you will never really start your work. You will remain buried under a heap of insignificant things, while infinite space lies open before you.

Stop making everything revolve around you, your partner, your children, your friends and neighbours. Do you think the stars are interested in your family life or your social life? It's up to you to turn your attention to the stars, and everyone will feel better for it.

20 June

Before a building can be said to exist, it has to be built; we must be able to see it. But really, its true creator is the architect, the person who drew up the plans for it. Even if the building is not yet visible and tangible, it's already been created in someone's head. Now all that remains is to build it, in other words to bring it into form with the use of different materials. Formation is always preceded by creation, which takes place high above in the world of ideas, sometimes instantaneously.

God created the world in an instant. It was the formation that took time; with formation time appeared. That is why we speak of the six days of creation. These six days are symbolic, of course; they represent the time it took for formation. Creation is instantaneous; it belongs to eternity.

21 June

The archangel Uriel presides over summer, the season of maturity. Uriel is fire, warmth and flame. The trees have already been in flower for a long time, and these flowers must produce fruit. But what is a flower? It is the organ of the plant that's closest to the animal kingdom. This animal-like part of the plant possesses sensibility and something similar to a nervous system: it opens to the light and closes in the dark.

We could go even further and say the plant's astral body is formed within the flower. In fact, the flower is the plant's sexual organ, where fertilization takes place. So, the archangel Uriel works with warmth to enable flowers to produce fruit.

22 June

How many spiritualists abandon their work when they find they don't get immediate results! It's not that the teaching they received is unsound, however, or that they have been given ineffective methods; it's that they haven't known how to proceed correctly. And above all, they are in a hurry, because they are lazy and very soon tire of making any effort. They've been living under the illusion that there are ways of overcoming difficulties quickly. Well, it's not the case!

Of course, that's how it happens a bit with medicine: you take some tablets, have a few injections, and there you are, back on your feet. Unfortunately, spiritual work is completely different: there are no tablets, no injections there; you have to undertake a lengthy work on the matter of your own being. You must cook it, knead it and fashion it. And anyone who claims to be able to reveal secrets that will transform you and your life in a short space of time is a charlatan. It is possible to receive the sudden revelation of a truth or of a new direction to take, but afterwards you must work and work. It is an enterprise that never ends.

23 June

The universe forms an immense unity in which everything is linked. So every physical object corresponds to something on the subtle planes, particularly on the astral plane. Mages base their activity on this law: they link a certain object with its corresponding current of forces; the object is used as an aid to mobilizing these forces.

An object made of beautiful material, with harmonious lines and beautiful colours, corresponds to something beneficial and life-giving on the subtle planes. Thanks to these forces, which are also represented by the divine virtues, you can use such an object to stir up the higher layers of the astral plane. While you are concentrating on these virtues and reinforcing their presence within you, this object allows you to contact beneficial forces, which will rain down on you and those around you.

24 June

The French use the expression 'to make love', but whoever invented it wasn't all that inspired. For no one can 'make' love. Love is a current of forces, way beyond us; we are not masters of these forces, still less their creators.

Love is a power, a principle that comes from God himself. It's an energy, and when we love it's this energy we allow to pass through us. But as humans rarely know how to love, this energy does not pass through them harmoniously. So they say they 'make love', by which they mean they assume certain positions, make certain gestures and say particular words… but is that love? It's doubtful.

25 June

Earth, water, air and fire, the four elements that constitute the matter of creation, are also a form of nourishment for us. Each day, we take solid and liquid food, and the air we breathe is also food for us. As for the element of fire, it is contained in these different forms of nourishment, but it is also found in sunlight. All creatures benefit from the sun's light, but most often unconsciously. If they did so consciously, they would find it a source of extraordinary wealth, for that is where our true nourishment lies.

Eating and breathing bring us life. But when we concentrate on the light of the rising sun, our soul and spirit are nourished by fire and light, and that's when we feel truly alive.

26 June

In order to bring movement to the motionless matter of stones, God created plants. Plants are intelligent entities, but their soul floats a long, long way from them in space. So we cannot communicate with them as we do with animals, or as we do to an even greater extent with humans, who are inhabited by an individual soul.

The first ray of God's love is manifested through plants. Plants are the first to bring life to inert matter, and they speak to it like this: 'Oh you creatures that live in stones, you have been there for billions of years, and you think you have been abandoned. But God thinks of you, and little by little you'll get back on the path of light again. It's a long way, but you will make it one day.' And they continue to work on the matter of the mineral kingdom, making it more supple and moist. Then along come the animals to continue this work of refinement. And then humans… This is how matter is enlivened, enriched and illuminated.

27 June

Unity is one of the conditions of life, and it can only be achieved if humans respect an order of things in which not only does the lower submit willingly to the higher but the activities of each person converge towards a summit or a centre. This order of things is called hierarchy.

This hierarchy also exists in us, from our feet up to our brain. Each of us forms a collective being, and if this being is to be harmonious and balanced all our organs must strive toward the same goal. They must work together and give their consent to the principle at the summit or centre: the spirit. Only then is unity created.

28 June

Although they are obviously unaware of it, many people become real enemies of humanity because of the deplorable way they live. And if you try to make them understand this, they retort, 'But what do you mean? The way I live is my own business, I'm free, I'm only harming myself'. Well, no, the fact is, when they go out and about and come into contact with other people they darken and poison the atmosphere, and their emanations also create disorder in others.

You must understand that, for evil as well as for good, there are no barriers between yourself and others. When you harm yourself you also harm the whole of humanity, for evil spreads in waves. And the same is true for good. So, when you purify yourself and when you seek light, all of humanity and even the entire universe benefit from it. Try to understand that, and you will feel you have no choice but to find the best direction for your life.

29 June

Many activities that humans engage in can be interpreted symbolically. Take dressmaking and embroidery for example. Both involve working with cloth, a needle and thread. 'Well,' you'll say. 'What's so interesting about that?'

For those who know how to interpret them, each of these three objects – thread, needle and cloth – corresponds to something within human beings. The thread is thought and the needle is the will, which engages thought. Plied by the will, thought carries out its work on the cloth: the physical plane. The needle and thread form pictures on the cloth that can be colourful or dull, harmonious or disharmonious, light or dark. These pictures depend upon a human being's intelligence, will and physical matter; they tell the story of a person's whole life.

30 June

Marriage is not just a human institution; it is a cosmic reality. For true marriage is that of spirit and matter. The whole of creation arises from this union. Each atom is the fruit of the marriage of spirit (energy) and matter. When the husband and wife are separated, as in nuclear fission, this separation pulverizes everything: the husband is furious and destroys his wife. When they are united, they live in peace and they create, but when they are separated by force they produce explosions.

Energy must unite with matter in order to fashion it, give it form. And as it's always the same original model that's reproduced exactly in a multitude of different guises throughout creation, all we see are marriages both in nature and in human societies.

1 July

Humans all have the same origin, and before they began their long journey far from their heavenly homeland they lived in the bosom of the Eternal. Consequently, they have retained a memory of this paradise, albeit as very distant glimmers. But during the course of their successive incarnations they haven't all had the same experiences: while some have strayed onto dark, tortuous paths, others have kept a clearer awareness deep inside themselves of their divine origin. This is why, when certain parts of initiatic Science are revealed to them, they say to themselves, 'Yes, that is the truth… I already knew that!'

As for those who have allowed themselves to be drawn into disorder and chaos, they are closed to all revelations. In order to rediscover these truths, they must try to take the path again that leads to the heights by purifying themselves, in other words by working on their thoughts and feelings with love and wisdom.

2 July

It is important that you pay attention to the quality of your food, but even more important is your psychic state when you eat, for you can poison yourself with even the healthiest food when you don't take certain precautions. How? If you are troubled by negative thoughts and feelings as you put food into your mouth, the food becomes impregnated with the poisons your thoughts and feelings are carrying, and it will disperse the poisons throughout your body. Yes indeed, you should know this: as you absorb your food, it becomes impregnated with the harmful elements you are sending out, and it poisons you. Of course, the opposite is also true.

It's normal to be momentarily upset or annoyed by certain events; but if that is the case, even if it's time for your meal, wait a while before eating until you have re-established inner peace and harmony. And if you cannot, if your commitments require you to eat immediately, at least make the effort to concentrate on your food and imbue it with your respect and your gratitude: as these feelings enter into you, the food becomes the medium for them, and they transform your negative states.

3 July

Say three times, 'God is light within me, the angels are warmth, human beings are kindness'. Then say three times, 'God is light within me, my spirit is warmth, and I am kindness'. These formulas given by the Master Peter Deunov are affirmations. 'I am kindness.' Yes, even an evil person will eventually become good if he repeats these words with conviction and with the sincere desire to improve. Humans will not know or understand anything of God unless they sense him inwardly as life, strength, love and light. True revelation lies in the sensation, the certainty, that the Lord is within us and that we are fused with him, that there is no separation between him and us.

These formulas from the Master Peter Deunov recall certain of Jesus' words which are also powerful affirmations: *'The Father and I are one'*, *'My Father is still working and I also am working'*, *'I am the resurrection and the life'*, *'I am the light of the world'*. These phrases spoken by Jesus represent the goal we too must attain if we are to become true sons and daughters of God.

4 July

When we see what humans call freedom, the word 'debauchery' would really be more appropriate. Why? Because they want to be free to give in to laziness, pleasure and passion, without realizing it's precisely this that limits and enslaves them.

True freedom is not acquired by freeing oneself from all constraints but by becoming a servant. Yes, but the servant of God, who is absolutely free. God is the only being in the universe who is truly free. He depends on nothing and on no one; it is he who consciously, willingly, limited himself through the act of creation. If you really want to be free, make yourself the servant of the Lord, and seek to merge with him; then his freedom will permeate you.

5 July

Our physical body is made of matter, and, because matter is subject to time, it wears out, decays and disintegrates. This is what we call ageing, and it's not very pleasant when we notice the evidence – the wrinkles, the white hair, the rheumatism and so on. But we are not just a physical body, and if it's in the natural order of things for the body to age we're not forced to age inwardly with it! So there's nothing much to worry about!

People who get so upset by the signs of ageing they notice in the mirror every day are generally already old inside. Instead of being concerned with maintaining what's warm and alive inside them – their heart – they identify with their body, with matter. But it is their heart, not their body, that determines whether they are young or old, and if their heart ages it's because they allow it to. In order not to age, you must conserve your love for people and things and never lose your curiosity or interest in the rich, abundant life that's all around you.

6 July

The bee is a symbol of the initiate, who has learnt to transform, sublimate and illuminate everything within himself for the preparation of honey. The beehive is within him, and the honey is all the purest and most subtle elements that radiate from his whole being: his emanations.

All beings are called to seek out and extract a quintessence from themselves, so as to transform it into honey. To do this they must work with their mind, heart and will, for it is thanks to these instruments that they can realize everything in their inner still. This is also true alchemy. The true alchemist has learnt one thing: how to become a bee and extract all that is best from nature and, above all, from human beings. He looks at them and speaks to them, and each one is a flower whose nectar he will collect in order to prepare honey.

7 July

Even in their spiritual life humans fail to detach themselves from matter. They visit holy places, go on pilgrimages and venerate relics, but by clinging in this way to places or material objects they will not succeed in touching the great beings who left their trace there. Instead of the spirit, they will find only antiquities and dust. Instead of life, they will find death.

Spirit alone gives life. As for relics, they can be compared to… tin cans! If you want to eat peas, or apricots or sardines, you can of course open a tin can. But these peas, apricots or sardines no longer contain the same life they had when they were freshly picked or caught. And this is even truer on the spiritual plane. So, leave the tin cans, and go to a restaurant that will always give you the freshest food: this restaurant is the sun. From the day you decide to frequent it, you will find the light, warmth and life that nourished the great beings you seek to trace.

8 July

You will always find people who claim it's impossible to know what's good and what's bad. They know perfectly well, really, but it suits them to pretend they don't: this way they can give in easily to all their impulses. If they reasoned a little, they would know whether they were going to act well or badly. Do they want, for example, to supplant someone, to belittle them in the eyes of other people, or to seduce them only to reject them later? Well, they should put themselves in the other person's situation and imagine what they themselves would feel if they were them. They will find out immediately how distressing, unfair and dishonest it is. How is it they've suddenly come to see the light? Nothing can justify those who claim not to know how they should behave.

Jesus said, *'Do to others as you would have them do to you'*. So, it's clear, is it not?

The day humans learn to weigh life's small contradictions against all the good that fate has generously dealt them, they will feel nothing but gratitude. Until then they will continue to torment themselves, comparing the so-called 'little' they possess with everything that those they see as more privileged possess. Well, these comparisons are invidious.

If you must make comparisons between yourself and others, why not see all the advantages you have, when so many human beings in the world have to suffer persecution, wars, epidemics and famine?

Ingratitude and constant discontentment are signs of a lack of intelligence. Why do so many people see only reasons for unhappiness, wherever they look, instead of realizing that heaven showers them with blessings?

10 July

Learn to contemplate the rising sun as if you were watching it for the first time. Say to it, 'Oh, dear sun, I didn't know you yet. I saw, of course, how beautiful you are and how you distribute your light and warmth each day, but I still hadn't understood the lesson you are giving us. Now I understand that you're showing us the path of truth, perfection and plenitude. I want to become like you.' Of course, you will never become like the sun; it's impossible, but that doesn't matter. Place the image of it in your head as an ideal, because it is precisely what is impossible that influences us, that strengthens and transforms us.

Yes, instil this truth firmly in your mind. Only what is impossible and unachievable can truly encourage us to progress, to constantly forge ahead, and this is why we must take the sun as an ideal to be attained.

11 July

Scientists are joining forces worldwide to alert public opinion to the risks run by humanity as a result of their pollution of the air, the water and the earth. But does anyone stop to consider that asphyxiating fumes, gas escapes and toxic products spread in the psychic world too? Many present-day illnesses are due not only to the pollution of air, water and food but to psychic pollution. If the psychic atmosphere we are immersed in were not so polluted, it would be easy to neutralize all external poisons. The ill is first and foremost inside. When you feel strong inside and in harmony with yourself and others, it's as if currents of energy were running through you, throwing off impurities – even on the physical plane – and your organism succeeds in defending itself better.

12 July

The earth is alive; it breathes, it eats, and like every creature that eats it also needs to eliminate, its eliminations sometimes manifesting as what are called volcanic eruptions. And since the earth is alive, it doesn't remain insensitive to the activities of the humans living on its surface as they endlessly transform and exploit it for their comfort. They turn it upside down, rummage around in it, dig it up or flatten it, without once asking themselves whether they are disrupting an order that they don't understand. The earth receives all this in the form of itches, stings and wounds, and then from time to time it gives a flick to rid itself of these disturbances. Humans must become aware that they live on the skin of the earth that supports them. It puts up with their actions for a few minutes – or a few thousand years, by its own timescale – but in the end it gets angry. Then they are terrified and they suffer, but will they be willing to learn the lesson?

13 July

Those people who wish to embrace the spiritual life, but who leave their old way of life prematurely, find themselves helpless and without protection. Then they say they were wrong to make that choice. Not at all. They simply lacked intelligence and foresight.

Observe how nature works: does it tear off an old skin before the new one has formed underneath? No. Well then, in the same way, you must still keep the old forms while you are creating new ones. Spend time creating the conditions that will allow the spirit to come and settle in you, and during this period stay with the old forms temporarily while you are preparing to leave them. That is wisdom!

14 July

What a lot of publicity and fuss there is at the moment concerning the needs of the physical body! All that matters is that you protect it, maintain it, take care of it, make it beautiful, dress it and adorn it. But to be preoccupied with one's body to this extent is dangerous.

Whatever you do, your body is and will remain vulnerable and perishable, and to found a whole culture on something that is destined to disappear so rapidly has deplorable consequences for all other activities. If people show so little wisdom, understanding and kindness, it's because they live with this obsession with the physical body. They don't know how to reason or act correctly, for the starting point is wrong: they are identified with the physical body. But if they concentrated on the needs of their soul and spirit, which escape the laws of time and space, everything they did from that point on would bear the seal of light and immortality, and this would be the coming of the kingdom of God.

15 July

True love is a vibration of extreme subtlety, and to be able to send out this vibration, as well as attract it, requires a great deal of attention and vigilance. Nothing is more important than knowing how to give and receive love. Those who have understood this feel such fulfilment and such joy that everything else pales beside it. For love is something quite different from the attraction that propels humans toward each other and then causes them to separate when the attraction ceases and they feel drawn to someone else.

The day you know what true love is, you will draw elements from each encounter that are purer, warmer and more luminous – immortal elements – and each one of you will say, 'My God, thank you! You have sent me a being who, for me, is like the sun that warms me and gives me light in the winter, a being who is like a delicious, sweet-smelling fruit that nourishes me, like water that quenches my thirst and air that lightens me.'

16 July

When an initiate opens his window in the morning, he greets all of nature, the sky, the sun... He wishes the day and all of creation a good morning. By this gesture of raising his hand, he enters into communication with the source of life. And nature responds to him. He greets the angels of the four elements: the angels of air, earth, water and fire, as well as the gnomes, undines, sylphs and salamanders, and then you'll see them singing and dancing: they're happy! And to the trees, the stones and the wind the initiate also says, 'Greetings! Greetings! Good morning!'

You, too, should think to greet nature in the morning: you'll feel something balancing and harmonizing within you. Much that is obscure and incomprehensible to you will leave you, quite simply because you will have taken the decision to make contact with living nature and all the creatures who inhabit it.

17 July

Prayer is based on the power of the spoken word, for the spoken word is an essential factor in realization. But, prior to this, the desire and thought should already be powerful on the spiritual plane. The spoken word is then like a signature which permits the release of forces from on high.

When you are praying, you wish to express a feeling of love and adoration towards the Creator: since feeling is purely psychic, you don't need to use words. But if you wish to achieve something on the physical plane, then the spoken word is necessary. However, the intensity of the thought and feeling remains what is most important.

18 July

Many people wonder whether angels really exist. Yes, they exist. They are immortal creatures made from such pure, subtle matter that nothing can reach them. They live in light and perfect joy, and they know everything except suffering. For suffering has a hold only over matter that is not absolutely pure. And an angel cannot suffer, because it is absolutely pure.

There are no angels on the physical plane; you will meet them only where the higher regions of the astral plane begin.* At the boundary between the lower and higher astral planes there extends an intermediate zone where beings who work to rid themselves of all impurities live. They are still susceptible to torment from negative influences on the lower astral and physical planes, but the moment they cross this zone they become like angels.

* See note and diagram p. 376-377.

19 July

Each day I speak to you about life, for the study of life, divine life, the life of our soul and spirit, is an endless science, which is what makes it so captivating. Once you have begun, you feel you will never be able to stop making new discoveries. This science of life is the only science really worth studying in depth, but at the moment it's disdained and scorned in favour of knowledge that isn't so essential. But what is scorned today will be appreciated tomorrow. The science of life is the stone of which Jesus says, '*The stone which the builders rejected has become the chief cornerstone.*'

20 July

If people seek to meddle in your affairs, to take your place, from a need to extend their territory or their influence, know that the possibility is always there for you to project yourself toward the heights or descend into the depths of your being. And once you are there, never let them in; defend yourself, for in your inner space dwells the Divinity.

It's not so much your personal interest, your egotistical rights, that you should defend, but you must defend the divine right within. And what does it mean to defend the divine right? Never be willing to infringe the rules of love, wisdom and truth by taking part in any venture that could impede your own path to perfection or that of others.

21 July

Many imagine that prayer, meditation and action are incompatible. Well, that's the biggest mistake there is! Many men and women of action have been true mystics. Oh, of course, there have also been many who were not, but what exactly have they done that's so good? Those who leap into action, without going first to seek light from the spirit, run the risk of producing nothing but disorder and destruction. Do you want to help others? Your action will be beneficial only if it is well directed. And how can it be well directed if you possess no inner resources or light? Even the best people with the best intentions will do little that's good if they rely on their own resources and their own inspiration. To be truly useful you must possess great spiritual riches.

22 July

How is it that we're able to move around easily on the earth? It's because the earth is hard and resistant. Try moving forward on quicksand, and you'll be swallowed up. And how is it that boats are able to move over water? Because water, too, is resistant, not as resistant as the earth, of course, but all the same it's thanks to the resistance of the liquid medium that boats go from one point to another. And it's also thanks to the resistance of air that planes are able to rise and fly in the sky.

So, you see, whether on the earth, on water or in the air, movement and the possibility of going forward are due to a certain form of resistance. And it's the same in the psychic domain. So, the day you understand that difficulties and obstacles represent a useful resistance, not only will you no longer complain, but you'll see in them only magnificent opportunities to advance. You will say, 'But I can refuse to go forward!' Yes, you can, but then you will be crushed, trampled underfoot. Because the law of life is to advance.

23 July

For many Christians, religion amounts to a series of articles of faith which bear no relation to their daily experience. They passively accept dogmas they have been inculcated with and don't know what to do with, and since they don't know what to do with them they continue to live like any other non-believer. This is how religion has ended up having little in common with true faith; only beliefs remain, and these will save no one. These people are Christians, of course, but if they won't work or make efforts or experiment, what result can they hope for?

And yet we are told in the Gospels that faith can move mountains. But as long as believers are content to repeat often unintelligible formulas, gestures and rituals, their faith will not move mountains or work any miracles. And when I speak of miracles, it's not about healing the sick or raising the dead, but about transforming oneself, bringing oneself back to life.

24 July

Life is none other than a form of combustion. It is impossible for anything to manifest in the universe without the combustion of matter to produce energy. And human beings cannot live, in other words cannot act, feel or think, unless a fuel is burnt within them to feed the process.

To sustain life, something must always be burnt. You will say, 'But what must be burnt?' Good question. Instead of burning your most precious quintessences by giving way to instincts and passions, learn to burn your instincts and passions by renouncing them. You must put your jealousy, anger and sensuality right there in the fire, the fire of the spirit, so they produce an extraordinary light, flame and heat, like the black, twisted branches that feed a furnace. The secret lies in how we burn all our impurities to feed the heavenly fire.

25 July

As the sun rises in the morning, little by little forms and colours begin to grow clearer. What the sun is, in this way, for nature and the physical world, divine light is for human consciousness. Lucidity and true thinking are given to human beings only if they make efforts to approach this light. The instant the light enters their consciousness, everything becomes clear, and they begin to perceive the true reality of things.

So, think of light; surround yourself with light, and introduce light into yourself. For light is also the most powerful of protections. Just as fire keeps wild animals away at night, so the ray of light you project with your thought repels the dark presences and currents that threaten your inner peace.

26 July

If humans had not understood the advantages of organizing themselves into societies, they would still be spending their days in the forests looking for food. As soon as they saw how useful it was to come together to pool several arms and legs, they benefited from this new situation, and now everybody is at the service of everyone else and can benefit from everything.

In reality, however, humans have resolved the problem of collective life only superficially. Externally, they may live organized into societies, but inside themselves they have remained isolated, separate, aggressive and hostile towards one another. This is why work still needs to be done inwardly, spiritually, if human beings are to succeed in forming a true ideal society, a universal brotherhood on earth. Then they will have attained the sublime consciousness of unity and will live in plenitude.

27 July

Nutrition is an inexhaustible subject, for it is concerned with the whole of our being. Everything we absorb teaches us its secrets. To know things and beings, you have to introduce them into yourself in order to study them. Nutrition is the key to knowledge: you must always begin by absorbing what you wish to know.

By requiring all creatures, even the most lowly, to feed themselves, cosmic Intelligence obliges them to acquire at least some rudimentary knowledge: as they eat they begin to study the nature of things. In order to develop and learn, one should always begin by tasting. And what is true for microbes is even truer for humans. But for humans, of course, eating is no longer limited to the physical plane. Their heart, mind, soul and spirit also need nourishment. When you pray, meditate, read and study, when you contemplate the colours and beauty of nature, when you listen to music, what are you doing if not nourishing yourself on the higher planes?

28 July

What is evolution? A change of form. In order to manifest, spirit always needs new forms, for form itself does not evolve and must be replaced. When we say time destroys everything, we mean only forms; time has no power over principles.

Forms are useful and necessary, but after a certain time even religions must abandon them in order to welcome new, purer, more elaborated ones. This is why Christianity should not seek to perpetuate forms inherited from the distant past; such an attitude goes against the decrees of cosmic Intelligence, which breaks up old forms to allow for the advent of new ones. So it should be of no surprise that the Church is being shaken up. Whatever it does, its old forms will be broken up. Christians must understand that the forms in which their religion was given to them centuries ago have lost their effectiveness and must be replaced, so that the content, the spirit of Christ, can be better expressed.

29 July

The earth lives, feels, breathes, thinks and evolves, and because of this it influences humans. The earth isn't mentioned in horoscopes; it isn't taken into account at all, and yet we are all influenced by the state and position the earth was in on the day we were born.

We are influenced more by the earth than by any other planet, because we are closest to it. Why does the moon have a greater influence on us than the sun? Because it's closer. And the earth, since it is our 'pied-à-terre' and therefore even closer to us, influences us even more through its different states. It has moments when it is awake and moments when it is asleep, as well as moments when it is thinking, when it is unhappy or when it is delighted. No one cares about the earth's different states. This is wrong, for we live in constant contact with it, and the currents that pass through it have a direct effect on us.

30 July

Love is an exchange between two energy currents, two opposite but complementary poles. It isn't the physical body that inspires love. This often intervenes only at the end of the process as an outcome; it merely follows on. What inspires love is invisible.

Generally, we give more importance to the body than it really has. Do the corpses of two people who have loved each other embrace when they are placed side by side? No, but their souls, which are alive, continue to meet. It is the life within creatures that provokes attraction or repulsion. So, before their bodies become attracted to one another, fluidic currents have already been drawing them closer. Their bodies merely follow this movement right at the end.

31 July

Spiritual practice is difficult, of course, but is made still more so by the fact that those who decide to devote themselves to it don't know how to establish the right inner attitude. There they are, in a hurry, tense at the thought of the numerous other things they have to do, and they can't manage to put all these concerns to one side. In their unconscious, in their subconscious, there's something that blocks them and stops them from getting results.

Obviously, these days, life, with its greater speed and the many imposed obligations, does not favour spiritual activities, which require us to know how to free ourselves from our daily concerns and find another, more harmonious, rhythm. But those who acquire the habit of fulfilling certain conditions for inner peace, for half an hour or an hour, will not only succeed in linking to the world of light but will then carry out all their professional and family obligations with greater ease. Everything must be done in the right place and at the right time.

1 August

All those who awaken to the spiritual life are visited by luminous spirits from the invisible world. These spirits are like gardeners who come into their orchard to pick fruit and enjoy eating it. They say, 'Oh! This watermelon, this melon, this peach… what wonderful fruit!' And they take an interest in these people, delighting in everything luminous, musical and perfumed emanating from them. You can all be visited by celestial gardeners. You may say, 'But I have nothing to give; I'm not an orchard. How can anyone come looking for something from me?' In fact, there's always some useful element to draw on – even medicines can be produced from poisonous plants! Humans have no inkling that, because they are like laboratories full of chemical elements, they are constantly being visited by creatures from the other world. They would be better off if they weren't full of poisons, but even their poisons are taken and used.

2 August

Knowing how to live collectively is the way ahead for true human evolution. Yes, you do not evolve by remaining alone in your corner, reading, learning and developing. When you isolate yourself in this way, you merely give free rein to your egotistical tendencies. You should love community, the sensation of being immersed in a sea of souls, all vibrating together. Of course, some seek out community to fulfil their need to assert themselves over others, to make slaves of them and exploit them. The fact that you are looking for community does not of itself mean that you know how to live in it; it's often quite the opposite!

So, living in community implies a great deal of work, necessary work. Sooner or later everyone must conquer their self-centred tendencies: their egotism, ambition, greed or authoritarian nature, which cause them to come into continual conflict with others. Eventually they must be able to say, 'I am a collective being.'

3 August

Jesus said: *'So when you see the desolating sacrilege spoken of by the prophet Daniel, let him who is on the housetop not go down to take what is in his house.'* Not go down from the housetop… In the eternal language of symbols, the roof is the spirit, where one is always safe and at peace. Jesus' advice therefore concerns the psychic life. When troubles erupt in the world or within yourself, never seek help from below, but make the effort to climb as high as possible and remain there at the top; in other words, reflect, reason and link to heaven to find peace and light. Only in this way will you see clearly and find the means to act and save yourself and others, too.

How often has it happened that, instead of fleeing a fire, people have thrown themselves into it! Why? Because they've 'gone down' from the roof, lost their head and allowed themselves to become overwhelmed by worry and emotion.

4 August

The alchemists' motto is *ora et labora,* which means 'pray and work'. Yes, pray first, and then work. Why? So that they can direct their work in the best way, for, if work makes for greater and nobler human beings, not all work is of equal value and neither are all the goals that you set yourself in your work. You should know for whom and what you are working. Because it connects us to the divine world, prayer alone brings us light and gives direction to our activities.

Thanks to prayer, light is shed on what we have to do, allowing us to use our energies for the benefit of all. Some people claim that work is prayer. Yes, that is true in one respect, but all the same it is better to pray before working.

5 August

True nakedness is the one and only sign of truth. Yes, only truth is naked. So that you may rise within yourself to the place where truth is laid bare, each of you must become free of everything inside that is opaque and impervious to the divine world. When you achieve this nakedness, you can go very high and receive messages, advice, wisdom, love and God's help. You must stand quite naked before heaven, that is to say, stripped of your greed, your self-interest and your false ideas. The more you strip away, the higher you rise. Then, when you come back down – and you always do have to come back down, because as long as you are on the earth you have to perform your earthly tasks – you dress yourself again, that is to say, you again take up your activities, your projects, your relationships with your family, friends and neighbours and so on. It is necessary to clothe oneself for the world, but not for heaven: heaven loves only 'naked' beings.

6 August

You must never stop working and making efforts; you must constantly exercise your will. Yes, what is lacking so often is the will! Humans understand where 'good' is; they hope for it, they desire it, they aspire to it… But it stops there; they don't go any further or really put their will to work to achieve the good they approve of and desire, and they continue to live as they have always done, instinctually, mechanically and negligently. Daily life, of course, requires a minimal use of the will: getting out of bed in the morning, going to work, taking care of one's family and so on, but that is what everyone does; there is no great merit in it.

The will of which I speak is a decision of the heart and mind, themselves inspired by the soul and spirit. Do you wish to develop your will? Begin by studying yourself, so that you know yourself well. Then, decide to orient yourself inwardly in the best way, one that requires you to develop your qualities and correct your faults.

7 August

The starry sky is one of the greatest wonders of nature. But there are different ways of looking at the stars. You can take a map of the sky and an astronomy book, which gives a detailed description of everything known about the stars and the planets. This is certainly very useful for your understanding of the universe. But what will all that do for your soul and your spirit?

More importantly, how different those experiences are from the ones you can have when you're contemplating the starry sky, when your only concern is to merge with this immensity! A peace slowly permeates you, lifting you up; your only desire is to tear yourself from the earth and be transported far away into space, so you can relate to the spiritual entities of which the stars are the physical manifestations. In the regions where you are projected, you feel that nothing is more important than to unite yourself with the cosmic Spirit, to let yourself be penetrated by it, so you can arrive at a true understanding of things, an understanding that permeates all your cells.

8 August

The invisible world is as populous as the visible world. And in the places where humans live, thousands of luminous or dark entities come and go, circulating without being seen. If people do not dedicate their house or surround themselves with a barrier of light, the dark entities, finding the doors open, will enter and create havoc.

In nature all creatures are mistrustful: birds, animals and insects erect obstacles around themselves to prevent others from finding and capturing them. And human beings, who have also learnt to protect themselves on the physical plane, do not suspect that they are in just as much danger, and in fact even more so, on the psychic plane: a multitude of malign spirits try desperately, day and night, to destroy humanity. Fortunately, humanity also has protectors, entities that are luminous and full of love. Thanks to them, humanity has still not been destroyed, but we must work consciously to help them protect us.

9 August

Every day courts impose fines and prison sentences for theft and material damage. And, meanwhile, the greatest criminals walk free. Yes, they do! If you break your neighbour's windows or trespass on their land, or if you steal something from a shop, the wheels of justice are immediately set in motion to punish you. But if you cause someone to lose their faith, their hope or their love because of words you write or say or the example you set, or if you drag them into a life of debauchery or violence, then justice will leave you alone. And if you are a philosopher, writer or film-maker, the general public will even applaud your talent and award you a prize. When what is most precious in humankind is sullied, people are not particularly shocked.

So that is how humans understand justice: those who dare to touch their neighbour's material possessions are punished, but if they destroy their neighbour's psychic health it's of no consequence, because the soul and spirit don't count; what counts is their physical body and their purse!

10 August

Even if people who are miserable can take some comfort in the thought of not being alone in their suffering, telling them when they are in tears that you understand and share their sadness is not enough to really help them. And instead of adopting the same long face as they do, you should do the opposite and nurture within yourself such great faith and so much joy that these neutralize their pain. You have friends you want to help… Don't be receptive to their negative states, but go inside yourself to meditate on joy, and then return to shower it on them. You say it's impossible not to share in your friends' suffering, nor to show them you're doing it. No, if you love your friends, give thanks to heaven and earth, and project yourself all the way to the throne of God. Then, all the luminous beings in the invisible world will part to let you through, saying, 'Let's allow this person to come up, because they carry an irresistible love in their heart, and we must help them to make this love a reality.'

11 August

The mission of human beings is to transform matter through the power of the spirit. But so many men and women still remain numb and fixed, a bit like stones! The characteristic of stones is their inability to move; they have to be constantly pushed and made to shift. Then, one day, they're broken up by great blows from a hammer and turned into roads, bridges, houses and so on.

Everyone should at least try to leave the mineral kingdom, to become a plant and grow and later learn how to move. Look at all the advantages there are in being able to be autonomous. Animals can look for food, escape danger, and shelter from bad weather. Humans will have made great progress when they develop these possibilities in their inner life. But it will still remain for them to gain real access to the human kingdom, in other words, to the world of thought and reason, so they can become master of their own destiny.

12 August

Lots of people work for ideas, but what are these ideas worth? Spiritualists, though, work for a divine idea, one that is sustaining and rewarding. Since this idea relates to heaven, it represents a whole world and takes it upon itself to bring them hope, enthusiasm and joy.

Even if your different activities bring you a lot of money or the esteem of others, as long as you do not work for a divine idea you will not be happy, because you will not be linked to heaven. But work for a divine idea, and you will not even need to be recognized or thanked for what you do, as you will always feel fulfilled. So, put a divine idea inside your head; work for a divine idea, and you will see what this idea will do for you: it will even prolong your life. Yes, nothing is more stimulating or exalting than a divine idea. Believe me, I am speaking of something that I have constantly proved to be true.

13 August

If gold possesses real value, it's because it comes from the sun; it is condensed sunlight. The sun produces etheric gold, and the earth fixes it: for billions of years its rays have travelled through space and penetrated to the depths of the earth, where entities work to turn it into matter. And now we mine gold here, just as in summer we pick ripe fruit from a tree.

Humans fight for gold and kill each other for gold, but that is not what the sun wants. The sun wants to realize something good and glorious in them through the medium of gold. Ever since they first saw the sun shining overhead, they should have understood its plans and learnt to use the beneficial forces with which gold is replete, not only for their physical health but also for the flowering of their spiritual bodies. For it is possible to trace the course of the condensation process of gold back to the light, warmth and power of the sun.

14 August

The intellect is situated between spirit and matter. So, when we see matter impeding, blocking the divine impulses of spirit, our intellect can intervene to restore the spirit's force and open doors for it. The spirit is always pushing from the inside, but we are not always aware of it. Why? Because we do not call on the intellect. It is the intellect that decides and tells us whether we are facilitating the work of the spirit within us or else opposing it by giving matter greater possibilities. An enlightened mind is an extremely useful instrument; it discerns and judges impeccably.

Contrary to what some people imagine, the great spiritual masters do not reject the intellect, for they know that human beings have the capacity to use it to determine how best to act. They even insist that human beings be aware of the role the intellect has to play in supporting the work of the spirit on matter

15 August

It is said in the scriptures that *'the fear of the Lord is the beginning of wisdom'*. To understand this notion properly, one should begin by distinguishing between fearing and feeling afraid. Feeling afraid is an instinct which comes from the physiological depths of one's being and may have no objective basis. Fearing, however, has a mental dimension: when you fear something or someone, you know why.

According to what is written, it is fear of the Lord, rather than feeling afraid of the Lord, that is the beginning of wisdom. We must not be afraid of the Lord. He does not wish us any harm, quite the opposite. But we should fear not respecting his laws. This fear, then, is a consequence of understanding that the universe that God created obeys sovereign laws and that when we transgress these laws we only harm ourselves, for in doing so we contradict the cosmic order.

16 August

To call someone a specialist is to recognize his or her great skills, and it cannot be denied that specialization has been the cause of fantastic progress. In order to further their knowledge in their own field, specialists have to limit their scope of investigation. This is fine, but it is important, then, for them to see the relationship between their limited subject of study and the whole of creation.

What is it that 'specialists' do, anyway? They detach a small piece of bark from the cosmic Tree, the Tree of Life, and when they have thoroughly weighed it and dissected it they write books about it, bring together hundreds of people – their colleagues and students – and give a lecture in which they present their conclusions. And that is what they call 'science'. But once this piece has been cut off, it is, in a sense, dead! Since it has been removed from universal life, it's dead, not physically perhaps, but dead from the point of view of cosmic life. How can they then speak of the science of life?

17 August

Sometimes you tell yourself, 'Oh! I should have been more patient!' But it's too late, and the fact is, at the point where you explode with anger or indignation, you always find an excuse for yourself. So begin by never looking to justify yourself when you lose patience. Then, concentrate on this virtue, and think of what some people have had to endure during the course of their life. Study how they have reacted, and take them as your example. Patience is one of the good qualities of Saturn. Saturn is the old man who has lived through a great deal, meditated a great deal and understood a great deal. Obviously, you can't ask children to be particularly patient; it's a quality that comes with age, great age even. When an elderly person is impatient, it shows they haven't learnt a great deal in life. People's wisdom is measured by their capacity to endure things.

18 August

Those who unjustly accuse others of dishonesty and infidelity ought to know that, actually, they're pushing them to commit what they accuse them of. A man, for example, accuses his wife of betraying him. It's not true, and she protests and justifies herself. But it's no good; her husband is pathologically jealous and makes endless scenes: 'Where were you? Who were you meeting? Why did you look at so-and-so? Why did you say that?' He sees proof of her infidelity everywhere. And then, after a while, what happens? His wife, who has never wanted to betray her husband, eventually does just that, and she is the first to be amazed; she doesn't understand what led her to commit adultery. Quite simply, it was her husband who drove her to it! By continually suggesting it, he created favourable conditions on the astral plane, and the poor woman succumbed. He did everything to ensure what he said would eventually come true. This is how humans often unconsciously create the misfortune that befalls them.

19 August

On the roads we see a constant stream of cars passing each other as they travel in opposite directions. This opposition is normal, provided the cars don't collide. In our body, too, the circulation of venous and arterial blood flows in two opposite directions, but the two must not be mixed, as this is what causes the blue disease. So evil does not reside in the fact that opposing directions or forces exist, for these work together. But if these forces collide and mix, they eventually obliterate each other; this is what evil is.

Look again at fire and water. What extraordinary things can happen when we place water on fire! – but only when a partition separates them. Otherwise, the fire will cause the water to evaporate, and the water will extinguish the fire. This is what happens in all areas of life, when you don't know what to do to get opposite poles and contrary forces to participate together in the same work.

20 August

Strive to have an essential idea in your life, a divine ideal to which you are constantly linked, for by doing so you will be able to engage in your various activities without running the risk of dissipating your energies. Each activity is just one of the numerous forms or manifestations of the spirit. At the centre is the spirit, and everything must find its place in relation to this centre, for human life to be unified. In this way each activity contributes to the perfecting and blossoming of humankind.

True spirituality means that, whatever you are doing, you succeed in keeping your sights fixed on the spirit. Just as the brain controls all our physical functions, the spirit must control all our activities. The spirit has the right to disperse itself for the purpose of animating creation, but humans must walk toward unity. If they do not, dispersion, for them, means death.

21 August

Humans are always ready to experience things that will weigh them down and make them gloomy. If only they wouldn't go so far but could draw a few useful conclusions from the little they had lived! But no, they live their experiences to the full, and not just once but ten times, a hundred times! It never enters their head that they'll have no energy left for the day they may wish to try spiritual experiences. Why not? The day may eventually come when, disgusted at having thrown themselves into swamps, they'll decide to get to know purity and light. But it'll be impossible; they will no longer have either the means or the strength for it. If they imagine anything is possible, that they can rise to heaven, having descended for years into hell, it's because they know nothing about psychology or life. They have already failed, they are dirty, weighed down, listless – and they think they're going to travel the length and breadth of heaven? What naivety; what ignorance!

22 August

What we call trials are merely a series of problems during the course of our life that we have to resolve, just as schoolchildren or university students are given problems to solve and then given more difficult ones as they progress. Of course, the time always comes for them to leave school or university, but no one ever leaves the school of life.

So, the exercises and efforts humans have to make during the course of their life are endless. Instead of complaining and rebelling at having to bear yet another load and overcome yet another obstacle, they should first of all understand the cause and significance of these trials and then be glad they have new experiences to try and new truths to discover, for these experiences and truths are the only true riches.

23 August

What is peace? For most people the word conjures up the idea of a quiet life, away from everything that's aggressive. But peace is really very different from that; it's the most intense work in the world and can only be carried out by those who have understood that, first of all, it's an inner state. This state is the result of a victory, won after a brave struggle, over all the psychic conflicts that tear us apart.

Each day, in order for peace to reign within us, we must re-establish the connection between our consciousness and the spiritual centres in our brain and solar plexus. When we have achieved this, neither torments nor fears have any real hold over us. But we must hold firm to a fixed point inside; otherwise, nothing and no one outside ourselves can bring us peace.

24 August

You take it for granted that others should show wisdom, kindness and honesty and are indignant if they don't. But how do you yourself behave? You never ask yourself this, which is why there is so much chaos in the world. Everyone sees things the same way: they all expect others to be irreproachable, while they themselves can behave just as they wish.

Radio, television and newspapers are full of people criticizing and accusing others – it's all you'll ever hear, see or read. They make a career out of it, endlessly justifying their own mistakes. It's just the same in daily life: people always have something to blame others for, while they see themselves as faultless. But, in an initiatic school, you will see that the opposite is taught, that true work involves dealing with oneself, with one's shortcomings, deficiencies and mistakes – and in leaving other people alone!

25 August

When they rediscover their true solar origin, humans will realize that it's this same solar force that manifests throughout their body all the time: in their hands, their eyes, their brain and so on. Even sexual energy is of the same nature as solar energy. Cosmic Intelligence has conceived human beings in a divinely beautiful way. Yes, the perfect, ideal man and woman, as cosmic Intelligence conceived them in its workshops on high, are like the sun. This is why those who abuse the sexual force instead of understanding that it is imbued with the sanctity of the sun's light and that they can use it to create magnificent things deprive themselves of the most precious treasures. Even if this idea still seems incredible to you, accept it. It will encourage you to become more conscious, more master of yourself. It's a shame if you hear revelations such as these without their having a beneficial effect on you. Meditate on them, and hope to become like primordial man and woman, as they were when they left the workshops of the Lord, radiant like the sun.

26 August

Little by little, pleasure that is purely physical blunts sensitivity: you need more and more pleasure and stronger and stronger sensations in order to feel anything or find it at all satisfying. So it becomes increasingly difficult to be satisfied, because you become increasingly insensitive. This is borne out in all areas of life. If you consume too much food and drink, you eventually lose your sense of taste; if you accumulate sexual experience, you become blasé and contemptuous of your partners.

So try to reduce your physical pleasures a little, and seek more subtle experiences. You will become more and more sensitive, and the least sensation will provide the greatest joy.

27 August

Because humans do not know how to protect themselves, they allow all sorts of physical and psychic disorders to take hold of them. And the doctors who treat them, and who know no more about this area than they do, are content just to give medication. They never say to their patients, 'Close your door to dark entities, and live a purer life, so that you attract only heavenly entities.'

You will say, 'Entities? But what does that have to do with illness?' Have you read the Gospels? After Jesus had cured a sick man, he said to him, *'Go, and do not sin any more',* because faults and transgressions attract evil spirits by acting as bait and food for them. Once these spirits have entered a person, they cause a lot of damage, which leads to all sorts of physical and psychic disturbances. This is the reality doctors ought to study.

28 August

True life and death are not the life and death of the physical body. This is why the initiates tell us that only love brings us life and triumphs over death. If you wish to be alive, love!

But when will humans understand what love really is? They wait for it to happen, talk about it, say it's the most precious thing, that they prize it above all else, but the results of this love aren't great: instead of bringing life, it brings death, because they conceive of it in too limited a way.

People talk of a 'radical' remedy, meaning it's associated with the deep causes of the illness. Well, it could also be said that love is a radical power, since it touches the depth of a person's nature and transforms everything in them. It is love that opens all doors for you, that reveals the meaning and beauty of the universe. Above all, it is love that gives you the conviction you are immortal.

29 August

Vigilance is a quality never sufficiently emphasized – yes, being vigilant, keeping one's thoughts elevated, so as to discern dangers and avoid them. It's very obvious that when people are not vigilant and don't look, or else look without seeing, they can be taken unawares by anyone or anything!

Keep your eyes open, so you can be aware of what's happening all the time. But don't misunderstand me. I'm not talking here so much about your physical eyes or about what's happening outside you. It's not outside yourself that you're most exposed. You need to observe within yourself, so you can feel the currents, the states of consciousness, the feelings and the thoughts that pass through you. You will only be able to gain understanding of your inner life, and work for your liberation, if you keep your eyes open.

30 August

You have entered into a relationship with someone, and then one day you decide you have good reason to leave them. Relationships can be of different kinds, not just those of marriage. Of course, you can always leave someone, but only once you have given them what you owe them, according to the agreement you made previously. Otherwise, you will be forced by cosmic laws to find this person again, in this incarnation or the next, to finish discharging your debt. If you really don't want to see someone again, settle all your debts.

But this is a law most people don't want to recognize. As soon as someone no longer suits them, they cut the link in order to feel free. No, no; how many times already has karma forced humans to find their parents, their wives, husbands, friends, bosses or subordinates again in another incarnation, so they can repair the wrongs they have done them!

31 August

In your spiritual practice, get into the habit of concentrating on the image of the summit, on God himself. You will say Christians have been taught to address the saints, and each day of the year has one or several of them who respond to all the needs of humans. It is good to link to them, of course, but it's much, much better to concentrate on the highest point: the summit. For, from this summit you can release true powers; orders are then given on your behalf, and those who carry out the orders can be initiates, saints, prophets, the people around you, or even animals or birds.

In fact, the orders can be carried out by animals, or even by nature spirits or the four elements. But first of all you must rise to the highest possible point and address the Lord himself, and the Lord will give orders, which will be passed all the way down to you through a whole hierarchy of beings.

1 September

From time to time, you are sorely tempted to tell yourself, 'That's it! I've had enough of going to sunrises, doing the gymnastics and the breathing exercises, meditating, praying, watching what I think, watching what I feel and say. All this effort is exhausting; I need a rest.'

Of course, it's normal to have this sort of reaction. But when such thoughts come to you, do not open your soul to them. If you feel too tense, don't make the same demands on yourself every day, but you must never entertain the idea that you don't need to make any effort. It's effort that keeps you awake and alive. If you let yourself go for a moment, you will perhaps think that you are freer and more detached, but that won't last. You will very quickly feel heavy and stuck inside. So, beware!

2 September

Though wisdom and love may appear to conflict, in reality they work together. Wisdom concerns itself with little things and love with greater things. Wisdom affects only our minutest particles. Wisdom has never brought about drastic changes in human beings, whereas love can instantly transform their whole behaviour and often even their physical appearance, too.

So remember that the greatest transformations in the world occur not because of wisdom but because of love. Wisdom is useful, indispensable even, but only for giving direction. Only love makes things happen.

3 September

How many parables Jesus used to describe the kingdom of God! In one of these, he compares the kingdom of God to a merchant searching for pearls: *'On finding one pearl of great value, he went and sold all that he had and bought it.'* So, this merchant sold houses, furniture, jewellery, land and livestock to obtain a pearl. Does a pearl really cost that much? Yes, because it represents the teaching of Christ, the teaching of wisdom and light.

It's worth selling all we own to have this teaching, but only if we understand that 'selling' means being able to sacrifice all the non-essentials that weigh us down and encumber us. For, to be able to draw closer to divine truths, we must become detached and be stripped bare.

4 September

So many people have a materialistic idea of happiness! Even astrologers can be caught up in this way of thinking. When they have to say something about someone's destiny, they say, for example, 'Oh, it's amazing. You have Jupiter in the second house, the Sun in the tenth house and Venus in the seventh house. You will be rich, influential and lucky in love; it will all be yours.' Whereas, if your birth chart shows squares and oppositions or planets in fall or detriment, they'll conclude the future has nothing good in store for you. If, however, you present your horoscope to an initiate, he will look to see whether you have a high ideal and are capable of directing all your energy to serving the good. If this is the case, he will predict a magnificent destiny for you, without concerning himself with squares, oppositions or planets in fall, for he knows that you will be able to use your trials and failures to progress spiritually.

Present-day astrologers don't really have this same light, this different way of looking at things. They remain slaves to their ordinary mentality and judge things the way all materialists do. They don't understand that man's happiness depends on his capacity to place everything destiny has given him at the service of his spiritual progress.

5 September

World news, the most distant cosmic events and even the upheavals of vanished worlds reach us constantly, and we possess instruments inside us that record them. Of course, all this information remains in our subconscious, rarely reaching our conscious mind. You could say it's the same as for radio waves.

The fact that radios and televisions exist proves there is a mass of information circulating throughout space. These waves escape our conscious mind, but the appropriate instruments allow us to capture them. At this very moment, incalculable numbers of waves are travelling towards us through space from all corners of the earth as well as from other planets and constellations. These waves crisscross and become entangled without destroying one another. Each one can be captured by an instrument tuned to its frequency. These waves pass through us, too, but we don't feel them. Fortunately! For if our brain started to record, even for a moment, everything that takes place in the universe, it would be unbearable. It's important to know that waves are continually passing through us, and it's this that explains how we sometimes find ourselves in certain states without understanding the reason. This is why we must remain very vigilant.

6 September

As well as having a tendency to imitate others, most people also feel the need to affirm their differences. And often what happens is they imitate where they should be finding their own way and challenge where they should be looking for harmony. Well, it's precisely this challenging attitude that makes them most like everyone else!

If you really want to be different, you would do better to imitate the small minority of sages, who work only to bring peace and harmony into themselves and those around them. If you cultivate this way of being different, you will succeed in understanding human suffering, illness and anxiety, whereas all those people who resemble each other don't really understand one another. They have the same suffering, but, as they are concerned only with their own personal problems, they are incapable of putting themselves in other people's shoes. For they have imitated in them precisely what they should not: their whims, their egotism and their passions.

7 September

Before you start judging any difficulty or trial as being unfortunate, ask yourself, 'Is this really a misfortune? Isn't it good fortune disguised, instead?' As long as you do not ask this question, you will fight, rebel and derive no benefit from this difficulty, which was actually something good that you were unable to see as such.

Humans rarely know how to see what is good or bad for them. How many situations they consider beneficial are, in fact, real dangers! Yes, how often have the consequences of success been to lead people into catastrophic situations! And, on the other hand, obstacles and failure, for those who've known how to use them, have become the true cause of future success. Think about this, and try to accept this way of reasoning and seeing things.

8 September

God loves all creatures, and the symbol of this love is the sun, from which all creatures, without exception, receive the benefits of life, warmth and light. But the wolf uses the benefits of the sun to go and attack sheep, whereas the sheep prepare good milk. In the same way, while the criminal benefits from the sun to go and harm others, the saint thinks only of bringing them help.

The love of God, like the light, warmth and life of the sun, does not produce identical results in all beings: the saint and the criminal experience this love in totally different ways. If the criminal plots crimes, does this mean that God, the divine sun, inspires criminal acts? No, the criminal is misusing divine gifts.

9 September

The object you photograph does not appear at first on the film. For it to appear, the film has to be developed by being plunged into a liquid known as a developer. In the same way, everything taking place in the universe, and even on the farthest stars, is recorded in us as if on a film. Even when we are not looking or listening, everything around us is recorded. We don't as yet have the means to develop this 'film', but that doesn't alter the facts. Cosmic Intelligence has set things up in such a way that each atom in the universe is in communication with the whole, and what is true for an atom is even truer for human beings, who are made up of billions and billions of atoms.

We can know of all the events that take place in the universe, but it's up to us to work to develop the film, that is to say, our consciousness and sensitivity, so that one day we will succeed in reading the history of the cosmos.

10 September

'Nastradine Hodja, when will the world end?' his disciples asked him one day. 'But that's very simple; let's see now,' he replied. 'It will end when I die.' And, in a way, he was right; when someone dies, the whole world disappears with them, and when they are alive the world is also alive. There's something to think about! Yes, it depends on you, on your state of consciousness, as to whether the world is alive or dead, spiritual or material, subtle or gross, beautiful or ugly.

You will say, 'But we've known that for ages!' Well then, if you know it, why don't you manage to make it a reality? You know everything, yet you do nothing. Do something; resolve to change your inner glasses, so that the world and the people in it become truly alive for you.

11 September

Love contains all riches, but you will only truly find them when you have learnt to love. When two creatures discover their love for each other, why must they spoil it all so quickly? Why don't they understand that what's happening to them is the promise of the greatest happiness, the greatest fulfilment? – but only if they know how to use their glance, their words and all the subtle exchanges they develop between themselves, to become more perfect, purer and nobler. Obviously, that takes time. But, as soon as two people find they love each other, they can no longer keep their distance. And, just as quickly, they reject each other; they don't know each other anymore – because they moved too fast! You will say, 'Keep their distance? But why should they?' So that they can use all the currents emanating from them to elevate themselves, to be inspired and dazzle the whole world. Yes, so that you can say when you see them, 'But who are these two people? There's a light emanating from them, something divine.' For that is the purpose of love: to emanate light.

12 September

Daily life for humans is a continual movement to and fro between the inner and the outer: they're either leaving for work, going shopping or meeting someone, or they're coming back home again. If you were to interpret these comings and goings, you could say people leave the centre (their home) and go towards the periphery (their occupations and so on), and then they leave the periphery and return to the centre. Their motives for going out are of two kinds: either to take, earn or pilfer, or else to give, help and be useful.

The motives that humans have for leaving the house and going about their business fall into one of two categories. The thousands of possible nuances can always be summarized by the words 'to take' or 'to give'.

13 September

You follow a spiritual teaching and find the philosophy wonderful. Yes, but as long as you hesitate to put it into practice you will not understand it. If you are really nurturing the right thoughts in yourself, you will feel the need for your activities to match them. If you don't do this, it means you're not really very convinced. You shouldn't pretend. As long as you do not make what you know a reality, it means something is missing from your knowledge.

It's harmful to keep up the illusion with humans that there's nothing particularly shocking about not matching one's actions to one's thoughts. This is why a true initiatic teaching is concerned with all of a human being's faculties, all of their needs and the different activities that correspond to them. Initiation concerns the whole person: not just one's psychic activities but one's physical activities, too: how to eat, sleep, wash, walk, work…

14 September

Because the materialist philosophy is based on the only knowledge that human beings can obtain via their five senses – the knowledge of matter – it is not a true philosophy but one of appearances. Appearances are obviously real, but they do not show us all of reality, and we shouldn't be taken in by them.

Appearances act as a starting point for further reflection. They can be compared to Ariadne's thread, which we must follow if we are to find our way back through the labyrinth and out finally into the open air, into the light of the spirit. We need to work with appearances but not stop there. Those who allow themselves to be seduced by appearances face spiritual death and are devoured by the minotaur.

15 September

Behind their respectable, moral, even spiritual, façades, how many people nurture appalling thoughts, feelings and desires and behave like animals! Why put on this act, when they are accountable to celestial entities every day? If you gain the good opinion of these entities, everything in and around you will be wonderful, whereas if you are content to gain the good opinion of others by playacting you will be left with the same weaknesses and the same mediocrity. You will be subject to the whims of the crowd, who, on one day, can shout, *'Hosanna to the Son of David... Blessed is the one who comes in the name of the Lord!'* and, a few days later, *'Let him be crucified!'* as they did with Jesus.

Yes, we've seen this so often throughout history! Someone is glorified, and a short while later they're assassinated. Human nature is fickle and unfaithful, and if you rely on being appreciated you'll bring burning coals down on your head. Learn to rely only on the appreciation of heaven.

16 September

The laboratories in which scientists carry out their research are wonderfully equipped, but you should know that nature gave all of us a personal laboratory at birth – ourself: our own body, psyche, heart, mind, soul and spirit. So, the experiments you can engage in are not just those outside of you; each of you can carry out research and make discoveries deep inside yourself as well, using your sensations, feelings and thoughts.

Each of you must become aware that you possess an extraordinary laboratory within yourself; nothing is missing: all substances and elements are represented there, and you can work even better there than in the outer laboratories. Why? Because, despite technical progress, the instruments needed to discover all the elements that exist in nature have still not been successfully manufactured, whereas, within men and women, all the instruments and elements are already there at their disposal.

17 September

You receive inner answers to all your questions and all your prayers. If you do not hear the answers, it's because you have surrounded yourself with thick walls by indulging in thoughts, feelings, desires and actions not inspired by love, wisdom and truth. If you begin to knock these walls down, you will hear. Now, it may happen, of course, that you don't find it easy to accept the answer you receive. When you're wrestling with an insoluble situation and wondering how you can get out of it, you tend to imagine that a solution will appear as if by magic to extricate you from it. No, no, the solution may require enormous effort on your part. But don't back away, because, if it really is the solution, however painful, it's worth more than all the hesitation, uncertainty and anxiety you have been living with up until now, none of which will go away as long as you refuse to make any effort.

18 September

All human beings have been given the faculty of thought. But how do they think? If someone goes up to a pile of dung and starts moving it, it will emit a nauseous smell. Well, this is how people often think: they move the dung, and there's a foul smell! There isn't one human being who doesn't think, for thought precedes everything and presides over everything. Even those who do nothing think, but their thoughts drift like leaves in the wind. Others actively think how they can steal, deceive, pilfer, murder…

True thinking first involves knowing what to think about and how to think. For the initiates, thought is a means of allowing human beings to approach the divine world, the world of light, certainty and peace. So resolve to do this work; even if you are on your own and deprived of everything, you will live in joy, and heaven and earth will be within you and belong to you.

19 September

So many men and women feel like deposed kings or queens in exile! They are aware of their own true worth and think no one else recognizes it in them, and they suffer from the conditions they find themselves in: society has no regard for them. But what is society? It's a vast stage where all sorts of comedies are played out, but these comedies must never make you forget what is most essential, that the real 'you' is the one inside, not the show you put on on this stage. Keep faith only with the power of your spirit and the immensity of your soul. Do you need the regard of others so much? And even if you do become the object of their regard, do you know how long that will last? Human beings are so changeable, so fickle!

20 September

What people call love cannot, in truth, find complete satisfaction on the physical plane. For it is not the physical body that needs love but the heart and, beyond that, the soul and the spirit. Those who stop at the physical body can only experience a few sensations, a few pleasant emotions, which often turn into jealousy, aggression and even hate.

In love, as in many other domains, you must see the body not as the goal but purely as an instrument. All couples who live together without making the effort to seek something beyond physical pleasure gradually turn their lives into a hell, for they end up seeing only each other's negative points. If they really try to make their love an exchange at the level of the soul and spirit, they will taste renewed happiness each day. Even when they have grown old, they will never stop rediscovering each other and enjoying each other's company. For it's not the envelope – the receptacle, the body – that one loves but what it contains: the spiritual principle, born of the one, inexhaustible Source.

21 September

Listen to a violinist tuning their violin: they have to do it with absolute precision, not any higher or any lower than the fundamental note all instruments are tuned to. If they don't do this, they won't be accepted in the orchestra.

Human beings can be compared to a many-stringed instrument, or else to a building with many storeys, in which tenants of all kinds live side by side. These tenants, who are rarely in agreement with each other, come one after the other to say their piece. So, our first task is to see ourselves clearly and then to seek the fundamental note with which we can harmonize the strings of our instrument or the tenants of our building. We will find this note only if we persistently aim for the summit, the divine world.

22 September

For creation to become eloquent, alive and meaningful for you, you have to learn its language. Your whole life must be directed to this goal: to enter into communication with nature and its inhabitants. The inhabitants are everywhere: in the water, in the air, on the earth, in fire, in the mountains and trees, in the sun and the stars… everywhere! And they greet us and give us signs. But who sees them?

And who, also, sees nature as a luminous substance traversed by rays, whose colours and beauty no language can describe? If you wish these inhabitants to accept, help and support you, prepare yourself for entry into this immense world by giving it your attention, understanding and love. You already live in this world, you walk in it, but you must open your awareness still more to it and lift the veil that prevents you from seeing it.

23 September

Try to acquire the taste for working with the light: not just with sunlight but also with this invisible light that imbues all of creation, for only the light can re-establish order in you, can make all your cells vibrate in harmony and restore your health. It is light that possesses the greatest powers on the physical plane, just as on the psychic plane. It's not perhaps the fastest method, but its effects are permanent.

Think of the light more than you think of anything else in your life, for the extreme subtlety of its vibrations takes us closer to the world of the spirit. For at least a few minutes each day, think only of light and nothing else. It will be like a beam of pure particles passing through you. This beam will become so powerful it will touch all creatures on earth and awaken their divine nature.

24 September

Evolution is the law of life. Everything must evolve, even minerals; they evolve very slowly, but they do evolve. There is a force in minerals which works to bring to light all the qualities and virtues they contain. Precious stones and precious metals are more highly evolved minerals, possessing beneficial virtues. Plants also evolve, and the more they do the more they provide nutritious, healing flowers and fruits. It's the same with animals and people, and it's even true for our planet and the whole solar system.

Everything must progress and improve; where this law is impeded, destruction occurs. Entire human cultures, worlds and constellations have disappeared, because they have opposed the law of evolution. So, try to take this law seriously: your whole life will be transformed by it, and you will create a magnificent future for yourself.

25 September

Because of the enormous advances made by science, many scientists, thinkers and philosophers believe it could replace religion, which, as far as they are concerned, only stupefies human beings. Why not replace religion with science? That's fair enough, provided they can take science to another dimension and broaden the field of inquiry.

What was to stop science and religion from being two ways of looking at the same reality, with science focusing on the physical world and religion on the spiritual world, since man was made to live in both worlds simultaneously? All it would have taken was for people to be aware of the dual aspects of reality and not to want to favour one at the expense of the other. And yet, what the West has done over the course of the last few centuries is either reject science in the name of religion or else reject religion in the name of science. They haven't understood that the truth lay in the harmonious balance of the two. For the universe is a unity.

26 September

To really know people and things, it is not enough just to see them. Do we know the earth because we see it? Not at all. We don't know all its laboratories or the countless workers who work in them. Do we even know water just because we drink it, air because we breathe it or light because it shines in our eyes? No. That's only the physical side. The sun itself is known primarily as a source of light and warmth, but that's very little compared to what we are destined to know about it.

Jesus said: *'And this is eternal life, that they may know you, the only true God, and Jesus Christ whom you have sent.'* You may ask how one can know the Lord. It's not really a matter of objective knowing, for we're not separate from him. But, in order to know him, we must heighten the intensity of our vibrations, until we find the wavelength that corresponds to his and are able to identify with him in this way. For knowledge is none other than an alignment and fusion with the being that one wishes to know, in other words a harmony of vibrations.

You decide to do a retreat... For a fortnight, three weeks or a month, you're immersed in a spiritual atmosphere that helps you find yourself: you feel balanced and peaceful, your life's direction seems clearer to you, and so on. But this period inevitably comes to an end, and there you are back in your mundane reality, and the intensely luminous quality of what you have lived fades. This is inevitable, especially if you don't already have a spiritual practice. But you must make efforts to preserve the benefits of such a spiritual retreat for a little longer each time. So, say to yourself, 'I know I'll never be able to avoid returning to mundane life, but I must keep the luminous experiences I've had safe inside; they are what will protect me when difficulties arise and I feel discouraged. Whatever happens, I won't give up, I will not get downhearted and I will not lose my flame, my enthusiasm and my hope.'

28 September

It's easy for a few people to be united, to have good relationships and understand one another, for humans generally tend to group together according to their affinities. But when it's a question of all the countries and all the nations on earth having to live together, what problems there are! For centuries, millennia, they have risen up against each other with their own visions of the world and their different religions, with their different political and economic systems and their different traditions. How can they be brought into harmony? That requires a prodigious science.

You follow the teaching of the Universal White Brotherhood, and you think it's enough to meet together and maintain good fraternal relations. Well, it's not enough! Even if there are a few hundred of you or a few thousand, it's still not enough. The aim of our teaching is not to unite a few people but to unite all people. When you come here, that is what you should be thinking about, what you should be working towards: finding out what you can do to spread this philosophy of universality.

29 September

When autumn comes, the archangel Michael separates the fruit from the tree. With his sword, he severs the connections. But this separation must take place at the right moment, just as it must in childbirth. The child is like a fruit that detaches from its mother, the tree, and this separation must occur at exactly the right moment; the umbilical cord should not be cut prematurely.

In the same way, the Archangel Michael separates the human soul from the body, which is its husk. In a sense, the soul too is placed in the granary, in other words in a peaceful place in the invisible world, where there are no mice or diseases and where the master of the house watches over it. Later, it will be re-sown, in other words sent to earth to be reincarnated. Once again the soul will experience winter: it will suffer as it remembers nostalgically the place it has left, that place where peace and light reigned.

30 September

Since time immemorial, humans have seen animals as symbols of their dominant characteristics and qualities. You will find them in all religions and in numerous rites of initiation. Some are well known, like the snake, the fish, the bee, the dove, the cat, the cow, the ass, the ox, the wolf... others less so, like the hedgehog.

In some traditions, the hedgehog is one of the symbols of the initiate, because it is immune to snakebites. It feeds on slugs that destroy the garden, or, put another way, it makes the harmful larvae on the astral plane disappear. Lastly, its spines represent the spikes the initiate can use to break down the condensed fluids of negative thoughts and feelings.

This is why, in certain initiations where a disciple undergoes symbolic trials to overcome poison, when he emerges victorious he is called 'hedgehog'.

In our soul and spirit we are free, but this freedom is only available to us to the degree that we strengthen our links with heaven. Our freedom lies in submitting to God's plans, in not rebelling against difficulties and suffering or trying to avoid them, but in reflecting on them and understanding why they exist. Heaven may not change any of the events we must live through, but inwardly it will give us the chance to deal with them better, and we will therefore experience them less painfully.

The freedom we must seek is not on the material plane but on the plane of consciousness. If we accept what God, master of all destinies, sends us, and if we wish to work for him, he will allow us to go through our trials as sources of spiritual enrichment, and in this way we will truly begin the apprenticeship of our freedom.

2 October

The Master Peter Deunov once said, 'You complain of having an empty stomach, because you've had to make do with a quarter of a loaf of bread. It's not really your stomach that's empty but your head and heart. If you add a wise thought or a loving feeling to each mouthful, a quarter of a loaf contains enough salt to nourish you for a long time.'

Was the Master really telling us to make do with just a quarter of a loaf of bread a day? No, he simply wanted us to understand that quality is more important than quantity as far as nutrition is concerned. But true quality is hard to find; it's not supplied in any shop. Quality is a spiritual element which must come from us. We must eat sufficient food, and it must be healthy, but it's our job to add an element from ourselves to the simplest of food to give it flavour, for this flavour will be a source of energy and plenitude.

3 October

Money, presents, violence, spells and magic – none of these methods can force someone to love you. The soul and spirit are the daughter and son of God, and nothing and no one has the power to force them. Let's suppose that a man or woman, whose love you have tried to win through magic, finally succumbs. It's not really this person's soul that wants you. Your magic has attracted other creatures, who have entered this man or woman to love you through him or her. But be careful, for the creatures you have attracted are not luminous entities (luminous entities do not give in to these kinds of practice) but larvae or elementals. So they will love you perhaps, but their love will devour and drain you to such an extent you will later pay very dearly for the semblance of love you acquired in this way.

There is only one harmless way to make someone love you: never think anything bad about them, and send them only luminous, pure thoughts. Even if you are rebuffed, be patient, endure everything, and do everything you can to help them. If you really are attached to them, you will touch their soul sooner or later, and they will love you.

4 October

Those who do good are not always aware of their actions any more than those who do evil. Instinctively, without even thinking about it, they bring help and joy to others. But cosmic Intelligence wants men and women to be aware of the good and evil they do, so that they learn about the laws that govern the universe and their own lives. This is why it's necessary, after death, for those who have unwittingly done good to not only feel but also see and understand what they have done. For in this, too, there are things they must understand, if they are to persevere with even more conviction on the path of good.

It is not enough to act correctly; you should learn to act with an awareness of causes, for then you will understand how the laws governing the universe work. This is why, on entering the other world, human beings discover in detail not only the good they have done but also how this good has affected others, and this is a wonderful lesson.

5 October

You say you need friends that understand you, but you can't find this understanding anywhere. Ask yourself first what it is about you that you want them to understand. And even if it's your highest aspirations, why do you insist on others entering your heart and soul and knowing what's going on in them?

It should be enough to know you have the understanding and support of the angels, those luminous entities that populate space, and of God himself who created you. As for the rest – your feelings, your moods, your likes and dislikes – tell yourself that these are just a question of temperament, that everyone has them, and that it's not so important whether others are interested in them or understand them. And, anyway, are you sure you understand yourself well? No? And yet you want others to!

6 October

When faced with any difficulty that arises, get into the habit of first considering the best inner attitude to adopt, before you resort to any other solution. This is what will allow you to deal successfully with any situation. For example, begin by saying to yourself, 'There's nothing much to worry about, the problems will pass, they won't last.'

You are surprised. You don't think that method could be effective? But it can; the thought that our problems won't last is the very thing that helps us to bear them. And besides, it's true, just think about it: how often in the past have you had disappointments, sadness or problems which, at the time, appeared insurmountable, but now, when you look back on them, all seem so distant, virtually non-existent, and you wonder why you were so upset and desperate. Well then, since you have all had these experiences, don't you think it might be worth using this method?

7 October

You know the story of king Mithras, who was afraid of being poisoned by members of his entourage and so sought to immunize himself by progressive exposure to poisons. It's true that you can make yourself physically immune to poisons, but is it that necessary? In all probability, none of you run any risk of being poisoned, whereas each day you are all exposed to psychic poisons, and if you don't know how to respond to these you will succumb. So you must practise digesting all the poisons that stupid or wicked people may pour over you on the astral plane. It was these poisons Jesus referred to when he said: *'Blessed are you when people revile you and persecute you and utter all kinds of evil against you falsely...'* Then, whatever happens, rejoice, and heaven will rejoice on your account: you will have passed the test with flying colours.

A true disciple of Christ is one who knows how to neutralize the filth they receive, without uttering a word against God or man. And if they give way to a gesture of irritation, rebellion or revenge, they ought at least to look at themselves and say, 'This time I failed, but in future I'll try to transform my anger and impatience into gentleness, love and kindness.'

8 October

People tend to think that spirit and matter work against each other, but in reality they are constantly moving towards each other. Spirit descends towards matter, and matter ascends towards spirit. This is why human beings, who represent matter through the bonds tying them to the physical plane, must pursue the spirit, their own spirit, God.

A river that descends from the mountain summit has the right to divide into smaller tributaries to irrigate the land it crosses. And the sun, too, has the right to distribute its rays throughout space to nourish the life of the entire solar system. But we are here below, and instead of scattering our energies we must direct our whole being towards the centre, towards the summit, so that we're able to receive its life and force. One day perhaps, we too will have the right to become dispersed, like a river and like the sun, but only when we have become alive like them. When that happens, we shall be able to project our life, the life of the spirit, onto all creatures.

9 October

The word 'magic' immediately conjures up images of wands, talismans, black books and spells, but of themselves these things don't amount to very much. Why not? Because the most powerful magic is found in the heart. If the heart doesn't intervene to lend intensity to your words or gestures, they will remain ineffectual. But on the other hand, if you nourish true love in your heart, heaven will listen to you and fulfil your wishes, even if you don't say any formulas or make any gestures.

So, leave talismans and magic formulas alone, since they won't be much use to you, but pray with all your heart, and you'll get what you wish for.

10 October

One person, on being given a half-filled glass, will say it's half full, while another will say it's half empty. Objectively, it amounts to the same thing, but for a psychologist this reveals two different sorts of mentality. If you focus on what is full, you blossom. If you focus on what is empty, you injure yourself. This is a law of magic. When invalids think only of their illnesses, their state worsens, because each negative thought leads to disintegration. But if they think of health they will immediately feel an improvement.

Of course, many things are lacking in your life. And if you want to be deprived of even more things, think about deprivation and emptiness… But think that you are a son or daughter of God, and so much will improve as a result! What humans really lack are not favourable material conditions so much as a luminous, divine philosophy, the only thing that's capable of freeing them from their weaknesses and limitations.

11 October

Evolving is about being able to enlarge the sphere of your concerns and activities with each day that comes. But what do we find? Humans are concerned above all with their personal interests and slightly with those of their family and their country, all of which leads to so many misunderstandings.

Many people will say there is no greater ideal than to work for one's country. This is not so, because their country does not represent the whole. If everyone set to work solely for their country, it would inevitably lead to conflicts with other countries. When you concentrate exclusively on a part of the whole, you necessarily enter into conflict with other parts of the whole. World peace would require people to see things from the broadest, most universal perspective.

In order to evolve, you have to continually expand your point of view, open your heart to an increasing number of creatures and use all your will to make the universal family a reality.

12 October

Sometimes, at the theatre, an inconsiderate member of the audience will go and sit in the front row, hoping that no one will come and move them. But along comes an usherette who asks for their ticket and sends them to the gallery; then the person who has reserved the seat comes to take their place. Well, it's the same thing in life. Those who manage, by scheming, to get hold of the place reserved for a more worthy person will have to vacate it, one way or another, and those who stay modestly in the shadows may be called to fulfil the highest functions.

So if someone momentarily occupies the place which should be yours, don't worry. The 'usherette' will eventually come, and the usurper will be sent packing. Yes, in this great theatre of life, everyone receives a number corresponding to their rightful place. It is their task to find this number and to know how to interpret its significance for themselves.

13 October

Stones are living beings. Since the entire universe is alive with the life of God, stones are also alive, which means they are capable of joy and even thought. You will say that since, unlike plants, they haven't been given an etheric body, much less an astral or mental one, they are unable to think or experience joy. It's true, stones do not have an etheric body or an astral or mental body, and if we've placed them at the foot of the evolutionary ladder it's because their spiritual being is so distant from them there's no communication between them. Stones are the receptacle for a spiritual being, but as yet this spiritual being has not entered into them sufficiently for them to be enlivened.

So, what is it within the stone that thinks and rejoices? It is the spirit above, not the stone itself. When you move or break stones they rejoice, because they feel they are about to participate in the construction of something new.

14 October

Symbolically, the numbers 3 and 4 speak to us of two worlds ruled by their own laws: 3, the spirit, forever moving and 4, inert matter. All of life throughout the universe can be summarized by this opposition between 3 and 4. Take the example of the zodiac. The zodiac forms an unalterable whole: the constellations travel through cosmic space but at the same pace; no one overtakes another. It is the planets that constantly form different figures. In this sense, the zodiac could be said to represent our body and the planets our spirit. In the same way, the organs of our physical body are in a fixed position whereas, inside, the blood, fluids and impulses of our nervous system never stop circulating. But it's thought above all that possesses the faculty of movement: it is free, and space is wide open before it.

In nature, as in man, matter remains matter and spirit remains spirit; you mustn't confuse the two, but you must learn how one works on the other. Spirit, 3, works on 4, which is matter. When 3 and 4 are brought together they create 7, which represents a living creature in whom spirit and matter co-exist harmoniously.

15 October

For centuries Christians have repeated time and again that the flesh is weak; this is the reason they have despised the physical body. But what ignorance! In itself, the body is neutral, the intermediary through which we manifest our thoughts and feelings. It doesn't force us to commit all sorts of excess and madness. We can also undertake magnificent feats with our body as intermediary.

And I will even tell you our body is the best instrument we have for moving closer to God. Yes, when God created the physical body, he placed within it all the elements we need to find heavenly order and harmony. The structure of the human body is an open book which teaches us how to return to the Creator, for it is the reflection of his wisdom, goodness and beauty.

16 October

Why is it said the fearful will not enter the kingdom of God? Because even if you possess great virtues, these will not be enough to neutralize the damage caused by fear. Does that surprise you? Well, it shouldn't. How often we've seen fear block the expression of all good qualities! Look, for example, how much the fear of loneliness, poverty, public opinion, illness and death makes people cowardly, dishonest, egotistical and cruel. So much crime is committed by people afraid of losing something they're overly attached to! This is also why, in initiations of old, only those capable of conquering their fear were allowed access to knowledge of the mysteries.

17 October

Whether our feelings are positive (like joy, love and enthusiasm) or negative (like anxiety, hate and jealousy), we experience them not in our brain or our physical heart but in our solar plexus. So, when initiates sited what we commonly call 'the heart' in the solar plexus, they showed they had a better understanding of what anatomy and physiology truly are. And the same is true when they spoke of 'the intelligence of the heart'.

Our intellect, the brain's intelligence, doesn't really know how our organism functions, with all its chemical, physical processes: respiration, circulation, digestion, elimination and so on, and the reason it doesn't know is because it doesn't feel these things. These phenomena are extraordinarily important and complex, but only the solar plexus is aware of them, for it is the solar plexus they depend on. The solar plexus is at the heart of the human being, just as the sun is at the heart of the universe.

18 October

What power cosmic Intelligence has placed in the human hand! It is thanks to their hands that men and women have acquired everything they possess today. What would they have created without them? For the moment, of course, they use their hands to act only on the physical plane, which is not very much. There are many things to be achieved on planes they know nothing about. Cosmic Intelligence has created the human hand as a living being with its own brain, nervous system and stomach. And since each part of the cosmos corresponds to a part of our body, our hand is linked to the whole cosmos. Yes, just as our body is a reflection of the universe, our hand is a reflection of our body, so it too is related to the whole universe.

19 October

A man and woman often decide to live together when they believe they've discovered a certain affinity between them. Unfortunately, getting together sometimes shows them how far apart they are in reality, strangers even. In contrast a man and woman may feel they are always together even when a great physical distance separates them. So, which is more important: to feel the presence of someone who is not there or to be physically close and yet feel apart?

Humans would undoubtedly feel happier if they learned to live more in their inner world. When you really love someone, they are constantly with you inside, and you are with them in peace. When you absolutely insist on being with them physically, you run the constant risk of arguments and misunderstandings. Don't, of course, give up all meetings and contact on the physical plane, but give preference to cultivating the possibilities of your inner world.

20 October

Shooting an enemy with a revolver or pouring a few drops of poison into their glass, placing explosives or turning on the gas to blow up their house – that's easy. There's nothing to be proud of or boast about in that sort of victory.

True victory does not mean annihilating enemies. True victory means successfully turning enemies into friends. Be very clear about that. For then, instead of being surrounded by people who seek only to harm you, you'll be surrounded by those whose only thought is to help you. It's difficult, of course; not only does it require great work on yourself, which is the first difficulty, but then there is the even greater difficulty, the work you have to do on the other person to convince them you could be friends. But if you gain this kind of victory, it proves you live in the truth.

21 October

How many monks, ascetics or even simple believers have willingly inflicted all sorts of torments on themselves... 'to please God', as they thought! As if God took pleasure in seeing a human creature wounded and bleeding! Very few religions have not recommended this sort of practice, and some still do today. But it is time to understand that the Lord does not need human suffering. The age of flagellation, torment and martyrdom is over. Mistreating and mutilating one's body and risking one's life – these ways of sacrificing oneself to the Divine are unproductive.

True sacrifice lies in fraternal, disinterested love for all humans. Those who have understood the meaning and power of love do not need to inflict suffering on themselves: they will have plenty of that, sharing the suffering of all those who are unhappy! And the obstacles they will meet in their efforts to help them will provide even more opportunities for suffering! But faced with this suffering, they must not recoil: it is what will make them greater and nobler.

22 October

Some people, when they feel tense or about to lose patience, leave the house saying they are 'going for a walk' or 'getting some air'. Something warns them that, if they don't go elsewhere, the situation will become explosive. Sometimes, just drinking a glass of water or eating a piece of fruit is enough to change one's inner state. Yes, knowing how to make a shift is a whole science in itself.

How often you allow yourself to get disturbed by trivial inconveniences! It would be easy to rid yourself of these states through a shift in consciousness. And there are so many ways of doing this! You can also alter your inner state if you wash your hands consciously while concentrating on a word: light… harmony… beauty… love… Next, you pass your hands over your head and ears, and then wash them once more. Begin again several times if necessary. You will feel lighter, for everything that's weighing you down will leave through your fingertips.

23 October

When your personal interests are threatened, in other words your comfort, well-being or reputation, you must be patient; and not just be patient, but thank heaven for the opportunity to show how intelligent you are.

But, what do people do instead? They watch unmoved as the forces of evil carry out their work of destruction on others, but they mobilize a whole army when their own interests are threatened. For this, they will one day be severely judged. Divine Justice will reproach them: 'You protested against the slightest injustice done to yourself, and yet at the same time you remained impassive before the humiliations inflicted on others, so in some way you contributed to them.' And it won't do them any good trying to justify themselves by saying, 'I didn't know.' They should have known.

24 October

Humans began by living isolated from one another, with each family defending its little territory. Later they formed tribes, then nations, and societies functioned like living organisms; you could say they reached the physiological stage. So humanity became an immense organism, one in which each individual works for the good of the whole and the whole works for the individual. We call this 'trade', and of course it is progress of a sort.

But now it's necessary to go further and work for a human brotherhood: that implies love and an awareness of the deep connection that exists between people. This is the psychological stage. As long as human relationships are based on self-interest, in spite of everything humans stand to gain from it being this way they will feel that something is missing; their life will remain meaningless. They will only find this meaning if they succeed in cultivating a brotherly attitude, in other words if they come to understand that they must share their very best with others.

25 October

To be born means to become subject to the law of blessing. Birth gives human beings the opportunity to correct their past mistakes and develop the luminous powers latent within them.

A child only comes into the world because a man and a woman have united to love each other; it is their love which calls the child into life. At the moment of their birth, each human being receives a visit from God. I know full well that many children are not really children of love, but I'm speaking in general terms, dealing with principles. When men and women meet and think of becoming fathers and mothers, they don't begin by imagining their child will be the fruit of chance or the result of violence, or that they will have recourse to artificial means of reproduction. Deep down in their heart and soul, everyone understands birth to be the natural fruit of love.

26 October

The moment you wake up in the morning, think of all the creatures of light ascending and descending between earth and heaven. Your whole day will be illuminated. Link yourself to these creatures; contemplate them in your heart and soul. You will no longer be happy to lead a prosaic life, and in order to keep these entities close by you you'll become more and more aware of your thoughts and feelings.

Those who are unaware of the reality of the sublime regions and the entities that live there are satisfied with an ordinary life. But those who know this reality feel that everything humans usually value is almost nothing in comparison. Yes, even the greatest things produced by science, art and philosophy pale beside it. You should at least know of the existence of those regions inhabited by perfect creatures, so you understand how important it is to draw closer to them.

27 October

People say suffering educates humans. But since they suffer, why are they not wiser? When they are in the throes of anguish, they resolve never to make the same mistake, and they even pray to the Lord though they've never prayed before! But as soon as things improve a little, their good intentions are quickly forgotten. Yes, because suffering is not enough, and if they don't understand why they suffer or what they should do so as not to suffer anymore they fall back into the same weaknesses, the same mistakes, and they start to suffer again.

Those who suffer need light, so that the reasons for their suffering and the means to remedy it become clearer to them, and they also need love to feel comforted and encouraged. You can only relieve people's suffering if you know how to manifest wisdom and love when you're with them.

28 October

Those who succeed in elevating their consciousness to such a degree that they comprehend the works of God are able to discover the quintessence of all sacred books, for the truths these books contain are inscribed in the life of the universe and in their own life.

God himself is inaccessible, unfathomable, beyond all understanding, but he placed within us and within his created universe all the elements which would allow us to move closer to him and decipher some of his messages. The first of these messages is light, since it is by means of light that he manifested himself at the beginning of the world, when he said, '*Let there be light!*' So if we wish to hear God 'speak' to us, we must seek light, for it is through light that he speaks to all creatures.

29 October

After death, when human beings have left their physical body, they enter the lower astral plane*, where they are subjected to all the injustice and suffering they have inflicted on others. You will say, 'But what if they have done wrong involuntarily without realizing it?' In the eyes of cosmic Intelligence, ignorance is also unacceptable. But the aim of cosmic Intelligence is not revenge, nor even punishment; above all it wants humans to become conscious, and so it makes them experience the suffering they have inflicted on others, so that they can learn, understand and become perfect.

Some creatures cross this lower astral region very quickly, as they have not committed very serious faults; others remain there a long time, suffering. When this stage is over, they enter the higher astral region, where they feel joy and happiness proportionate to the good they have done, for they must also become aware of their good actions. If they have given others courage, hope and light, if they have awakened faith and love, they live these same states.

* See note and diagram p. 376-377.

30 October

'Know thyself'... Self-knowledge is a requisite of human evolution. But exploration of the inner world is difficult and doesn't take place without risks. This is where initiatic Science is so necessary, for it teaches us that before reaching the clear, luminous regions of consciousness – the causal, buddhic and atmic planes – we must cross the dark regions of the lower astral and mental planes, where we are continually at threat from illusions and distractions.* These regions can be likened to areas of fog and dust. The crude emotions of the heart correspond to fog and the distractions of the mind to dust. The danger, of course, lies in remaining there, for both dust and fog impede clear vision. So if we are to truly know ourselves, we must make every effort to cross these murky regions, with a view to reaching the spiritual summit, our higher Self.

* See note and diagram p. 376-377.

31 October

Height, depth and width: these three dimensions correspond to the development of the human being. Height is linked to thought, depth to feeling and width to activity. So we should not speak of profound thoughts but of elevated thoughts, nor of elevated feelings but of deep ones. As for activity, it must be broad and vast. During its growth, a tree develops in these three directions in succession. To begin with, the seed gives birth to a root, which goes down deep into the soil. The longer the root and the deeper it goes, the taller and broader the tree will be. Next, the trunk is formed and gradually gains in height. Once the depth of the roots and the height of the trunk have been established, the tree spreads its branches wide.

Human beings must grow the same way a tree does. They can only elevate their thoughts after deepening their feelings, and once their thoughts have become elevated they will be able to extend their activity outwards.

1 November

Even if no one appreciates the efforts you make to perfect yourself, don't let that discourage you; you are making these efforts for yourself, not for other people. You will keep all the spiritual riches you are now amassing when you come back to earth. In what form? In the form of more favourable conditions, which heaven will give you for your spiritual development.

If you see you are still not able to acquire a particular quality, or conquer a particular fault, or overcome a bad habit, tell yourself frankly, 'It's because I didn't make the efforts I should have in the past, and now everything is difficult.' That's what you must tell yourself, and then you must get to work at once. Yes, even if you only have a year to live, a single year, you should make a start, for in that short time considerable changes would take place.

2 November

It is natural to suffer when you lose people you have loved and admired and to try to find them again beyond death, but you have to know certain laws and respect these in order to do that. The only infallible way of meeting these people where they now are is to try to cultivate the same qualities you felt and appreciated in them while they were alive.

This is, of course, harder than asking a medium to call up their spirit or going to the cemetery to meditate at their grave, or looking at their photo while imagining all sorts of things. But if you really want to meet your loved ones again, there is no other solution than to look for them through their virtues, for such an encounter can only take place through the law of affinity. By developing the same qualities as theirs, you will find their spirit again, and they only truly exist in their spirit.

3 November

With the passing years, our physical body grows and develops, because life penetrates and animates it. Of course, the time comes for the body to stop growing, but right until the end of our life it doesn't stop changing, because the principle of life within us continues to penetrate it. We shape our own body with our mind, our heart and our will, and we remain linked to it by all sorts of subtle connections which give us the power to act upon it.

What conclusion can be drawn from this phenomenon? That in order to truly act on beings and objects, you have to penetrate them; you must never lose sight of this law. You may say, 'Why do I fail to influence such and such a person – a parent or friend, for example – when I would like to help?' Because you haven't learnt to penetrate other beings with your psychic energy. And that is the principle of magic.

4 November

Why tell someone you love them? You love them, that's enough. Love is felt and seen; in fact, it's the most difficult thing to hide – it is shown through how you look at someone, your gestures and your attitude, and it's not necessary to speak of it. Humans rely too much on the verbal or written expression of their love. Once they've spoken of it, they think that's settled the matter. Not at all; they speak of it over and over again, but their behaviour increasingly shows their love is fading.

You should guard your love as a very precious thing, the most precious thing, and not express it in words. In this way it gradually creates the greatest freedom in your soul, the greatest delight and magic. If you speak of it, you will soon get reactions from all sides which will create misunderstandings, and this will be a shame. Do not speak of your love, and it will live in you forever.

5 November

Lost civilizations and the history of humanity are certainly very interesting subjects, but that is not where you will find what is essential. The essential thing is the life that flows today. You can find Christ's tomb and go and kneel before it, but there wouldn't be much point, for Christ is no longer there in the tomb. The Christ is an immense river that flows in the universe, wherever there is life, wherever there is love.

And besides, out of all the Christians who go to Palestine to trace Jesus' footsteps, or even all the heads of churches, would many follow him if he came back today? Not only would they not recognize him, they would once more persecute him and call for his death. Why? Because they haven't fathomed the secrets of life and love.

6 November

Like a king who has to deal with insurrections, each human being is torn endlessly between all the contradictory wishes of his subjects (his cells), and their rebellions reflect very badly on him. In order to restore peace and harmony, he must tame the cells of his body, just as his distant ancestors tamed the dog, the cat and the horse, or as some wild animals – tigers, lions, bears, panthers – are tamed and made to work in circuses. Why should humans not do the same thing with their cells?

If animals, even wild ones, can be tamed and educated, humans can also educate their own wild animals, their cells, and get them to work together in a constructive way. But it takes a lot of work, a lot of willpower and, above all, a lot of love to do that. With your strength, patience and love you captivate and train them, and they place themselves at your service.

7 November

Everywhere people talk of nothing but changes. Again and again they say that changes are needed... And what are these changes? Always the same relentless struggles for power, money and honours... with some getting rid of others so they can take their place. No, real change will only take place when humans work to become more honest and noble, more masters of themselves... examples. But they are not interested in that. What is the use of improving? That's not what they need; they need positions and titles to satisfy their desires and their greed.

You will say, 'Yes, but if we have to follow your advice and only work to improve ourselves, to become examples, with the world the way it is, we'll be left on the bottom rung of the ladder somewhere, unknown and unrecognized.' What makes you draw such conclusions? If you truly become a source, a sun, even if you object or refuse, others will come and forcibly place you at the top to govern them. If that hasn't happened to you yet, it is because you don't deserve it, because you are not yet ready.

8 November

In the soil that we walk upon, there live beings that were once endowed with movement, feeling and thought but have so descended into matter that now we trample them underfoot. This is how we can explain Jesus' words: *'If salt has lost its taste, ... it is no longer good for anything, but is thrown out and trampled underfoot.'* All creatures that have lost their salt and abandoned the spirit are trampled underfoot. All societies, nations and families which have lost their salt are crushed. Why? So that they will be forced to find their flavour again.

Of course, this point of view will seem senseless to many, and no geologist or palaeontologist will accept it. And yet, it's true: we walk upon beings who once lost their salt. Whether or not you believe me doesn't make any difference. What do we know of the civilizations that preceded our own?

9 November

Each time you make use of light and heat, each time you act with wisdom and love, you form the philosopher's stone inside you, which transmutes all matter into gold. And that's when you become a true alchemist. So you do not have to look for the philosopher's stone anywhere other than inside yourself, for there is no philosopher's stone more powerful than the spirit. The day you attain that state of consciousness where you feel your spirit, your higher self, is an immortal, eternal principle, an indestructible entity travelling through space and penetrating every place, you will understand there is nothing more important than to use this power to work on matter, your own matter, to purify it, vivify it and enliven it.

The philosopher's stone is this spiritual quintessence which transforms everything into gold, into light, in yourself first of all but also in all the creatures around you, for all things increase and multiply. This is the sublime dimension of the philosopher's stone.

10 November

We will never be able to say that we know or possess the Truth. For in the same way that an organism is formed from millions and millions of cells, so the Truth, the eternal principle towards which we must strive, is made up of a multitude of partial truths. No words and no amount of studying can reveal this Truth that is the synthesis of all truths, and it will not just appear before us. We are only able to know truths that gradually move us closer to the sublime, perfect quintessence that is the Truth. These truths touch the many aspects of the different worlds: physical, astral, mental, causal, buddhic and atmic.* If you make the effort to study all these aspects seriously and patiently, perhaps one day in the distant future you will be able to glimpse this Truth which embraces the totality of existence.

* See note and diagram p. 376-377.

11 November

We see that, from the chemical point of view, water is the result of the combination of two gasses. The formula H_2O means that one molecule of water is composed of two atoms of hydrogen and one atom of oxygen. So hydrogen is 2, the number of the feminine principle, and oxygen is 1, the number of the masculine principle.

Water is therefore the child of an oxygen father and a hydrogen mother. Can we make sense of this mystery, of the claim that the meeting of two gasses, representing the element air, produces a liquid? Two gasses, symbols of the masculine and feminine principles, united by the fire of love, give birth to water. Compared with these gasses, with this subtle matter that forms water, water itself is relatively concrete and material, and it is this water that brings us life.

12 November

From the moment we slip into sleep, our soul moves away from our physical body and goes to join the universal soul. During the body's rest, an entire work of cleansing and purification takes place. On its return, the soul finds the house cleaned and washed, and it can take up its work again. If the soul did not leave the body in this way, we would die from poisoning and asphyxiation, because the work of cleansing could not be done. You will say, 'But why do we have these toxins and poisons?' Because life is a combustion. All the physical, emotional and mental activities we know as 'life' produce a release of forces, but they also leave behind rubbish which takes a while to be eliminated. So it is necessary for the soul to withdraw from the body so the cleansing can take place. This is how nature has resolved the problem of life.

13 November

It is always up to you whether you are influenced by something or not. Even infernal spirits cannot force you. Obviously, if you have no discernment, if you take no precautions and don't know how to protect yourself, they can have an influence on you. They present you with all kinds of bait, and if you swallow the hook you fall into their net, and after that they lead you, quietly and imperceptibly, to your ruin. God gave them this power... but only if you are weak, if your consciousness is not enlightened. Once you have allowed yourself to be drawn in the direction the dark spirits wish to take you, they have formidable powers over you. But it's you who are to blame. They are what they are; they're allowed to be tempters. It's up to you to be lucid and vigilant so as not to fall into their traps.

14 November

There are two sorts of tenant: those who are not very scrupulous and take no care of the apartment where they live, who damage the floor and leave marks on the walls and say, 'Who cares about the landlord!' and there are those, on the other hand, who make their home more beautiful, put up new pictures, replace the wallpaper and so on. In the same way, there are two categories of tenants, that is to say spirits, living within human beings themselves: some take possession in order to damage the dwelling, while others reinforce, clean and purify everything and make it more beautiful.

Each human being is a dwelling for entities of the invisible world, some of whom stay for a few minutes, some for months or years and still others for a whole lifetime. Recognizing them is a science in itself. Those who stay for a short time are generally the most spiritual. They arrive with lightning speed to deposit presents in us in the form of light, and then they leave, but their passing leaves traces which can last for eternity.

15 November

Once an evening is not enough to 'examine one's conscience', as they say. Several times a day, you should ask yourself, 'Let's see, how does my heart feel? Is this really love? And are my thoughts on the path of wisdom? Has an element slipped in that will cause me to make a mistake?' Each time you introduce elements of love and wisdom into your thoughts and feelings, you attain more truth. So, each time you progress, you take one step forward in your search for truth.

These aspects, these steps are infinite in number; this is why you have to find truth and, at the same time, continue to look for it. How? By linking yourself once and for all to the two irrefutable principles of love and wisdom while, at the same time, discovering each day the most suitable ways to put them into practice.

16 November

Wherever you are and whatever activities you are engaged in, your primary concern must be to create harmony, because harmony is the basis of creation. It is harmony between all the elements and all creatures that ensures the cohesion of the universe. So long as you do not understand the importance of harmony, you will continue to create dissonance and disorder, and then, even if you think you are building something useful and long-lasting, you will only be destroying.

You will say, 'But I've got this ability and that skill…' It's not enough to be skilled; it wouldn't even be enough if you were a genius. You must make sure your activity is in harmony with the forces of nature, with the luminous spirits of the invisible world, as well as with human beings.

17 November

In the language of symbols, the circle with the central point represents the universe sustained and animated by cosmic spirit. Between this central point, which is spirit, and the periphery, which is matter, continuous exchanges take place, and it is these exchanges that produce life. Matter is the receptacle for all riches, but it is spirit that animates it, works on it and organizes it so that all the possibilities it contains can manifest. When the circle is without its central point, it becomes the image of chaos.

This law can also be understood in our inner life. The worst thing a human being can do is cut the link with his or her centre, or spirit, and become nothing but a circle: unorganized matter, an arid land, a desert. In order to become an organized world, fertile land, we must always link ourselves to the central point, the spirit.

18 November

Who doesn't feel justified in criticizing and attacking people when they find their behaviour appalling? And it's true, it is right to rebel against certain behaviour. But people must also ask themselves whether there are not things more worth rebelling against. Instead of being constantly indignant about a certain situation, a certain individual or political party, why not rebel instead against your own weaknesses, your own mediocrity and vices? Yes, vent your indignation and disgust on these, and try hard to curb them.

If rebellion exists in the universe, it is because it has a role to play. But humans have not yet understood where, when, how or against whom or what to rebel. They must rebel, I agree, but against all the entities that have settled inside them, which deceive and gnaw away at them. These are their real enemies.

19 November

You must make the effort to awaken those powers in you that have become dormant from centuries of inertia and stagnation. You won't go anywhere with inertia; you won't open any door, release any force or stir any layer of your spiritual being into motion. So put your will to work, concentrate, meditate, pray and do exercises. The teaching gives you the best methods for overcoming the inertia of a mind and heart blocked by the darkness and the cold. Always seek to add something more to your life, something more luminous, something warmer. You can even communicate with inanimate objects through thought, sending them subtle vibrations which will beneficially stimulate all those who pass close by them, beginning with yourself.

20 November

In exceptional cases, parents may slap or smack their child; it can't do any harm. Except that, if they do, they must take care that their face doesn't express any negative feeling at that moment, because the child will quickly forget the slap or the smack but will never forget an angry look.

So, be careful! When a mother has to correct her child, she should remain in control of herself and show the child that it hurts her having to correct him in this way. She should say to him, 'You see, I don't want to slap you, but you force me to, because you have behaved badly.' And then, go ahead… smack him! Then, the child feels that it's his fault that his mother is forced to act as she does. He reflects on it and begins to understand there are laws that he mustn't break, and gradually this produces a great improvement in him.

21 November

You must be able to live with humans and maintain good relations with them. You should help and love them but at the same time try not to share their weaknesses, in order not to lose any of your convictions or your spiritual energy. In this way you will be able to give them a few rays from your heart and your soul, and you will have the joy of enlightening a few creatures on earth. But you must know that you will only achieve this through initiatic Science.

Those who think, 'I'm strong, I'll resist, I won't be sullied' are naïve. No one has ever managed to sail through life unharmed, unless they've possessed great knowledge and exerted themselves to develop a formidable will. Those who overestimate their own forces will succumb like the others, because the world is so very rich, so very seductive and full of traps that after a while people succumb, and when one door has opened, that's it, they allow themselves to be invaded. In order to conquer temptation, you must have initiatic Science.

22 November

Humans tend to form opinions about people and things based on appearances, and they imagine that such knowledge is enough. Well no, this is why life seems monotonous and empty to most of them: their understanding of reality is so narrow and superficial!

Take the way men and women usually consider each other. When they have lived as a couple for a while, they think they have nothing more to discover about each other; indeed this is why they don't discover anything any more and get bored. But they should seek the reason for this boredom in themselves, not others. They are closed to the currents of life, and so all of the subtle side of people, their soul and spirit, eludes them. People are alive, and nature is also alive, but in order to make contact with this life they must refine some of their faculties of perception.

23 November

True direction, true knowledge and true experience come from above. Since time immemorial, the initiates, the great masters of humanity, have continuously transmitted the same knowledge to their disciples: they teach that, from the atom to the archangels and all the way to God, life is one continuous hierarchy of beings all linked to each other, each one constituting one part of that immense living organism which is the universe.

We humans are found placed somewhere on this ladder of creatures. Above and below us are beings that are linked to us. This link exists, whether we know it or not and whether we wish it or not. But it's essential for us to be conscious of this and to work at relating to the beings above us, who will take us with them, higher and higher.

24 November

A man and woman who love one another do not know what drew them together. They are aware of feeling an attraction but unaware of what gave rise to it. So what is the origin of that attraction which gives rise to love? Two beings, two energies meet in space; mysterious fluidic exchanges are magnetically developed between them. It is this meeting that gives birth to love, with each receiving from the other the elements they lack in themselves and have been unable to find anywhere else.

People are often surprised by the links that are formed between certain people; on the face of it, nothing should have drawn them together. Well, the explanation lies precisely in those subtle exchanges taking place between them without their knowledge.

25 November

You will have seen artists who were greatly admired but were living debauched and perverted lives, with their circle of family and friends wondering how they could express heaven in the way they did when their lives were hell. They themselves didn't know either. They were unaware that their gifts originated from luminous beings in the invisible world, who had come to manifest within them in the hope of saving them. Yes, the mysterious talent revealed in certain people is a sort of bridge which spiritual entities establish between these people and heaven. The entities write, paint, compose, sing and play through the people they inhabit, making enormous sacrifices to lead them out of hell. If they persevere on their path of destruction, the entities one day end up leaving them; they do so with sadness, but they have no alternative.

26 November

You will only master your inner world if you seek to identify with your spirit by placing it at the centre of your life as the sole stable, unchanging and indestructible reality. Gradually you will sense that you radiate in all directions of space, and a pure, powerful aura will form around you attracting the presence of celestial entities. Only those who succeed in forming a circle of light around themselves have truly found their place in the world. For wherever they go, the circle that surrounds them also gives them the very best conditions to create. In the same way that your physical body is protected by your skin, so your psychic bodies are protected by your aura. When you leave the centre, it's as if the aura, this spiritual skin, cracks, and the slightest annoyance makes you lose your equilibrium and your peace. The centre, your spirit, is your only true place.

27 November

Like the fish in the sea, the mole in the earth, the bird in the air and, so they say, the salamander in the fire, each creature must find its place. And where is the human being's place? The entire universe. The different organisms which make up this universe are linked to the four elements: our body to the earth, our heart to water, our mind to air, and our soul and spirit to fire.

Of course, it is desirable to find your place in a family, country and profession, but that's not enough. If your heart, mind, soul and spirit do not also find the place where they will receive the food they need, you will always feel dissatisfied. The heart needs warmth, love; the mind needs light, wisdom; the soul needs immensity and the spirit eternity.

28 November

The sky is grey... You would very much like to receive the warmth and light of the sun, but it's impossible. You have to wait for the clouds to go away, and while you are waiting you have the impression the sun has abandoned you. Not at all; it's just that you are below the clouds. Take a plane so you can rise above the clouds: nothing can intervene between you and the sun anymore; it's there, and it's shining non-stop.

If you feel abandoned inside, it proves you've come down too far below the clouds, and once you've done that, of course, there's always a screen depriving you of the benefits of the spiritual sun. Well then, since the feeling of being or not being abandoned depends on you, why not change your state of consciousness? Why remain in such a low place, where every minute of every day a screen intercepts the light? Who is preventing you from climbing up to receive the sun's blessings?

29 November

The cross is one of the simplest geometrical figures: a horizontal line and a vertical line intersect at right angles. But let's study the two directions. The horizontal direction is one of spreading and dispersion, like water spreading out over a surface. In contrast, the vertical direction is one of unification, like fire leaping up into the sky. There is something about fire's form that recalls the shape of a mountain with its base and summit.

So the horizontal line is that of matter, the vertical line that of spirit. And these two lines are not separate; they meet, or, to be precise, they 'cross', and this shows not only that the two directions are not incompatible but also that they have something to do together. The symbol of the cross invites us, therefore, to continue to carry out our work on matter and, at the same time, take the vertical direction, in order to return to the spirit, the source, the summit.

30 November

Do not look outside yourself so much any more for your happiness, for most of what you need is within you, in your inner world. I will even go so far as to say that, in the future, humans will be able to condense their inner world and make it appear as matter: they will know how to create what they need on the physical plane and give it form and consistency. Yes, just as God created the world, men and women will be able to create their external world. For the moment, they are at the mercy of the external world; they are subject to it. They do not have the necessary impulse to remedy the situation, to confront it, and they are overwhelmed. If something good turns up for them from the outside, they feel some small satisfaction, but if there's nothing they feel poor and deprived. It's not a grand state of affairs!

Prepare yourself for a future in which you will be master of yourself to such an extent that you will be able to make the outer world reflect your inner world. Then, your life will be splendid, immense and all-powerful.

1 December

All those who think only of increasing their bank balance, their social influence and their power over others are, in reality, only limiting themselves inwardly. And even if, at first, they derive great satisfaction from these things, they will be forced at some time or another to limit themselves outwardly, too.

As for those who walk the path of spiritual growth, they become free, even if they cannot avoid a certain amount of suffering and limitation. Their suffering resembles that of a mother bringing a baby into the world. This child is the fruit of a long maturation period, and its arrival often takes place in the midst of pain, but what joy there is when it's finally here! It is this experience that inspired Christianity to teach that the goal of spiritual life is for each of us to give birth to the Christ-child within.

2 December

Why are people so helpless when faced with life events? Because they are careless and thoughtless. They believe they'll be the strongest, and then they are victims! They are like those who would believe they can fight winter or prevent it from coming. One day they would be forced to admit that winter is more powerful than they are. They have to live through it, and what will happen if they've made no provision for it?

Never forget that winter will come, and tell yourself, 'I'm going to stock up with wood, coal and clothes, in other words with wisdom and love, and when I have these winter will be welcome!' This way, both winter and yourself will be happy. So that is the best attitude to have: don't fight against the trials fate deals you, but show how far-sighted you are, and strengthen yourself with wisdom and love, so you can face your difficulties with lucidity and courage.

3 December

'Our Father in heaven...' By teaching humans to think of God as their Father, Jesus changed the image they had of him. He led them out of a world governed exclusively by justice, into one of love, goodness and forgiveness. They were no longer the servants of an inflexible, implacable master but the children of a loving, merciful Father.

This change in the way people saw the relationship between themselves and the Lord brought with it another even deeper change, also mentioned in the Gospels but not yet fully understood. This change in perspective concerns the nature of human beings themselves. If God is our Father, we are of the same nature as him. You'll never see a father and his children be of a different nature. And if we are of the same nature as God, we can identify with him. This is why Jesus also said, *'Be perfect, therefore, as your heavenly Father is perfect.'*

4 December

At first sight there doesn't seem to be much relationship between water, wine, blood and love, and yet they have the same symbolic significance and play the same role in the universe. In the same way that water is essential to the earth and to the vegetation that covers its surface, blood is essential to our body and irrigates all its organs. You can drink love just as you would drink water or wine (that's when you feel inebriated by it!) or, like blood, love sustains your vital energy. In fact, love can be understood on all planes: it is water on the physical plane, wine on the psychic plane and blood on the spiritual plane; it brings life, purity and immortality.

5 December

Your ability to be happy at other people's good fortune is the criterion for how evolved you are. For, you must admit, it's usually difficult to be thrilled about other people's successes and happiness, especially if they succeed where you have failed. On the other hand, when you see them unhappy, it arouses kind thoughts and feelings, pity, compassion and the need to comfort them and help them. Yes, when others have accidents or serious illnesses and can no longer arouse envy in them, people naturally become more kind and understanding, without even having to try. So you must study your reactions to other people's success and happiness. The day you are able to be sincerely pleased for them will be the proof that you have succeeded in detaching yourself from the astral and mental planes* – your egocentric feelings and thoughts – and have been able to rise to the causal and buddhic planes where wisdom and love reign, which alone are capable of giving you true joy.

* See note and diagram p. 376-377.

6 December

Fear is not often mentioned as one of man's weaknesses, yet it is a great enemy of inner progress. It is very often fear that is behind cowardice, avarice and wickedness. You meet people who claim to fear nothing, but what do they mean by that? In reality, if they knew how to analyse themselves better, they would notice they are afraid of at least one thing or one person.

It's impossible to even count the different forms of fear: they are infinite in number, from the fear of accidents, illness and death to the fear of public opinion, lack of money or being deceived by one's wife or husband, and so on. Fear accompanies human beings throughout their life and obscures their inner sky. So every person must be ready to face it at every moment.

7 December

How disappointing it is for the young artists who have been idolized by the crowds to see themselves quickly forgotten and replaced by others! But however much they torment themselves and complain of life's unfairness, that's how it is: the public is pitiless and looks for novelty, and those it applauds one minute are quickly replaced by new people, and those by other new people – unless they know the secret of how to renew the life inside them.

If you know how to radiate new life each day, life that is love, light and purity, no one will ever want to replace you, even if you live to be 300! The sun cannot be replaced; all kinds of things and people are replaced, but no one as yet has ever managed to replace the sun. Husbands replace their wives and wives their husbands for all sorts of reasons. But the real reason is that all these husbands and wives have allowed their life to stagnate. No one wants to replace people who radiate life, for life is what everyone needs most.

8 December

Those who do not place heaven at the centre of their life live a life of anarchy. You will say, 'But I'm not an anarchist, in fact I'm against anarchy, and besides I'm not bothered about heaven, I don't believe in it.' This is perhaps intellectually true, but deep down you live in anarchy, for what really matters to you? Perhaps you will say it's the good of the community, the brotherhood of humankind, for nowadays everyone claims to think altruistically about the whole world. But let's see how you go about it. Have you really mobilized your thoughts, feelings and energies in this direction?

If you are honest, you will be forced to admit you are driven in all directions; you go wherever you think you can find pleasure, satisfy your ambition or get more money or honours. Well, that is true anarchy: inner anarchy. It's the state most people live in until they have learnt to mobilize and coordinate all their energies and place them at the service of a divine ideal.

9 December

Everything you experience in your inner life is fraught with consequences. Why? Because the nature of each thought, feeling and desire is to attract corresponding matter from space. Thus, good thoughts, good feelings and good desires that are supported by a firm will attract particles of pure, eternal, incorruptible matter.

If you work each day to attract this matter, it will enter you and find a home in you, and at the same time it will chase away all the old dull, sickly particles, until your physical, etheric, astral and mental bodies are completely renewed.* And as each particle of matter is linked to a corresponding force, the purer the matter the more it vibrates and attracts forces that correspond to its nature. So, when you replace the ageing particles in your organism with new, purer particles, you attract currents and forces from the heavenly regions.

* See note and diagram p. 376-377.

10 December

Several times during their existence, human beings have to undergo trials which force them to ask themselves the only questions of real importance: those concerning the meaning of their life. And if they are told they will find the answers in religion, most will continue to feel empty and lost.

But from time to time, certain people who are overwhelmed by suffering plunge so deeply inside themselves they find the answers right there. It's not religion that helps them, it's not faith that helps them, and yet they find faith because of what they are experiencing. For the truth is, God has placed in men and women all the answers to the questions they ask themselves and all the resources they need to confront the trials of life. Through trial and error, they can eventually find them, and they find them even more surely than in some of the explanations given them by religion.

11 December

The Master Peter Deunov used to say, 'If someone climbs onto your back, be patient; if they hurl swarms of flies and mosquitoes at you, you must also be patient. But if they place their hands over your eyes as you start off on your path, you must not accept it.' What does this mean? In our daily life, we must strive to carry the burdens others place on our back, and we must also be patient if they complicate our life and treat us unfairly. The only thing we must not accept is if they prevent us from seeing the right path and following it. We should not be patient with those who, through their words or behaviour, try to destroy the temple of God within us, to extinguish our light and cut our ties with the Creator. We should resist such people with all our force.

12 December

You can try to heal physical illnesses through psychic means: through thought, prayer and so on, but that will take a long time, even in the best cases. And besides, there is often no time to wait for a cure, and then you have to use material means: medication and operations.

However, in the long term, the only means that are permanently effective are spiritual ones. If you learn how to organize your life from the point of view of the soul and spirit, it will take you years, but in the long run you will succeed in establishing order and harmony, even on the physical plane. All material phenomena have their origin above, and the physical body obeys; it shapes and fashions itself according to the directives it receives from our thoughts and feelings and even our soul and spirit. As we are living on the physical plane, we cannot neglect the means of the physical plane; but at the same time we must give priority to the spirit, to thought, in the knowledge that doing so will one day bring about great transformations, even on the physical plane.

13 December

You don't become an educator by following courses or reading books on education. You can only become an educator if you were born an educator: then, merely by your presence, the looks you give and your emanations, you have a beneficial effect on the children. There have been people throughout history who were born with this love and these moral qualities; they influenced children through their natural authority and worked wonders with them. Children are sensitive; they can tell from miles away whether you're a master or not. Animals, too. Take the horse, for instance: if its rider is a coward, the horse senses it, then up it goes, and the rider's on the ground! Otherwise, it's submissive. Children also have this natural intuition.

Actually, true education is none other than initiation. A true educator is an initiate. Through their example, self-denial, patience and sacrifice, great initiates have slowly educated humanity, showing it new paths.

14 December

You work for an ideal, you are selfless and generous, and of course you risk being abused by other people or shown a lack of gratitude. So the time comes when you feel tempted to say to yourself, 'I'm an idiot, I'm so stupid, I should have realized beforehand that life is a jungle. To get success and respect you can't have too many scruples. Oh, how stupid I've been! But that's all over, from now on I'll act like everyone else.' Well, that's the worst kind of reasoning there is. It's painful to lose one's illusions... I know that as well as anyone! But why lose your ideal along with them or, in other words, why lose the only thing that can give your life real meaning? Whenever you are disappointed with human beings, from now on, cry for a bit if you can't help it, but never think you were wrong to follow the divine path of kindness, generosity and sacrifice: keep going!

15 December

Whatever their religion, all those attached to beliefs and rituals that take them away from the essential reality of light, warmth and life are the cause of great misfortune. If only they would turn to the sun to learn its lessons! The sun says, 'Look at me. I'm constantly sending you my riches; surely you can do the same.' But, in order to force their notion of God on others even though not one of them has seen him, humans prefer to massacre each other until there's no one left. And, actually, no one has ever seen God, but the sun gives us the best image of him.

The sun is the best expression of divine perfection. It distributes light, warmth and life to all and isn't bothered about knowing whether someone is Orthodox, Catholic, Protestant, Jewish, Muslim or Buddhist. For the sun, everyone is a child of God. Sooner or later, humans will no longer be able to ignore this reality, and they will find the one true religion. Then, even Christians will understand that Christ is none other than the spirit of the sun. They will feel the Lord himself, full of love, present in the sun.

16 December

Once they have reached a higher degree of evolution, certain souls, on returning to earth, make a solemn promise before heavenly entities to accomplish a mission. They promise to develop the faculties and virtues they already possess in order to help and enlighten humans. Whatever form this promise takes, it can be summarized as follows: they promise to place their qualities and their spiritual and material potential at the service of others. You will say, 'But don't all souls that come to earth have a mission to fulfil? Do some incarnate without a particular purpose?' You have to understand that all human beings are sons and daughters of God, and this imposes certain obligations on them, but not all souls have achieved the same degree of evolution. Many are still weak and inexperienced; they come down to learn and perfect themselves. For the moment, that is their only true mission, and that is already a great deal.

17 December

God distributes his love everywhere in the universe and in his creatures, but in order to truly benefit from it you have to learn how to attract it; you have to find the right attitude. It involves a great transformation in your spiritual state and demands that you become more and more sensitive to the subtle side of things.

As soon as you learn to nourish yourself with God's love, he transforms everything in your life. You are no longer dependent on circumstances; you feel free, rich and fulfilled. Whether others love you or not, you soar above everything, because this love is part of you and imbues the whole substance of your being. You will say this is hard to understand. Yes, of course it's hard, but it will be easy once you attempt to communicate with this subtle, living, profound reality, with the only thing that can fulfil you: the love of God.

18 December

The Creator gave us a will, so that we would make it the instrument of our higher nature and place it at the service of a high ideal. We must begin by understanding some essential truths. When you have understood an essential truth, use your will to put it into practice, in the knowledge that this is the only real way to understand it.

It's easy to spout truths; anyone can read the works of certain sages and repeat parrot fashion what they find there. By doing this, they may even win the respect of those people who are so blind they can't see how weak and feeble they are inside. But fooling the blind isn't much of an achievement! In any case, there are others who cannot be fooled: the luminous entities of the invisible world. And what's more, it's precisely these entities whose esteem we need to gain, and we will gain it by applying the truths revealed by initiates. These truths are weapons; we will never find better ones to help us triumph over life's difficulties, but we need an arm to make use of them; in other words, we need the will to put them into practice.

19 December

Success is obviously more pleasant and glorious than failure. But in fact, whether you are successful or unsuccessful, it isn't easy to find the right inner attitude. When people are successful, they may believe they're allowed to do anything, and when they're not they sometimes collapse. Well, the only thing to do is to attach little importance to either situation. What matters most is that we learn to use our faculties to deepen the inner link we have with our heavenly Father.

If other people recognize our faculties and benefit from them, so much the better, but that's another matter and not what should concern us. Our task is to develop ourselves in a balanced and harmonious way, so that we move closer and closer to the image of the Creator we carry imprinted within ourselves. For, to tell the truth, those who possess intellectual or artistic gifts are not necessarily any happier for it, if they do not use them to find this divine imprint.

20 December

All those materialists who have never done anything to make their inner world habitable think only of amusing themselves in the outer world. As soon as they find themselves in their own company they're bored; it's inner poverty. Spiritualists, on the other hand, know how to make their inner world so orderly and beautiful it lacks nothing: poetry, colours, music... everything that's beautiful is there, and they suffer when they are forced to 'go out' and leave this beauty behind.

So now, think about it... How much time do you spend with others? A few minutes, a few hours. And how much time do you spend with yourself? All the time, day and night. Well, don't you think it's much more important to improve the place you never go out of? Why do you allow your inner space to get so run down, like a hovel, or like an attic where the windows are broken, where spiders are walking across the ceiling and the mice are having a great time.

21 December

The seed of a tree that's been placed in the earth contains the tree in potential. No one could tell from it where the roots and stem are, let alone the leaves, flowers and fruit, and yet they will soon all see the light of day.

The seed is under the influence of the Archangel Gabriel, who condenses and solidifies elements. It is placed in the ground during the darkest, coldest time of the year, and Gabriel transmits memory to it, in the form of hereditary genes, which maintain its characteristics from one generation to another. He puts all the plant's specific qualities and virtues into the seed and condenses them into this minuscule mass, which contains all that it will potentially become. And he does the same thing with the semen of animals and humans. The specific characteristics of each generation are preserved in its chromosomes. The memory is not lost.

22 December

Initiation is a victory over the four elements: earth, water, air and fire. But, these days, initiation takes place not in temples but in everyday life, for the four elements are all present in daily life, and that's where you have to confront them and show that you've conquered fear, greed, egotism, sensuality and so on. Often, you fail over next to nothing, because you were expecting great trials: you didn't notice when a little problem arose, and you stumbled.

When you are forewarned that you will have to confront great difficulties, you are better armed and more resilient, because you know what to expect. But when you are caught unawares, you can fall at the first hurdle. So it's up to you to be constantly alert and vigilant, knowing that any of life's circumstances can become an initiatic test.

23 December

The human soul has a need for the magical, and the 'unreal' is in fact more real than what we usually consider to be reality. Many people must recognize, if they're truthful, that fairytales send them into raptures, for a brief time at least. Why? Because everything in the tales is not only alive but animate and endowed with speech: rocks, flowers, trees, animals... And the forces of nature act in them with intelligence. But above all, behind the apparent naivety of these tales are portrayed the realities of our inner life.

When, in certain very particular circumstances, something subtle, unreal and magical irrupts into our life, we feel like a tree that was once torn from the ground and transplanted somewhere in a hostile environment that now suddenly rediscovers its native forest, where it can once more take root and live again.

24 December

True evolution is a continuous ascent. But during the course of this ascent, each person will inevitably pass through highs and lows, and ups and downs; it's important to know this so that you persevere and don't lose courage. One day, there will be more ups than downs, and, as a loving father, God pardons those of his children who recognize their mistakes and decide to correct them.

It is impossible to reach the top without experiencing failure. The most important thing, though, is that you are on the path to the heights, the path of love and wisdom, which leads to truth. If you happen to take a few steps back on this path, it's not so serious. The main thing is that you keep going in the same direction, that you keep the same goal and the same ideal inside you and always fix your sight on reaching the summit.

25 December

Time, like space, has four cardinal points, which are the two equinoxes and two solstices of the year.

The winter solstice takes place on 21 December and is presided over by the Archangel Gabriel. And on 25 December, the feast of Christmas celebrates a birth, in other words a concretization, a descent into matter. The Archangel Gabriel directs forces whose specific task is the condensing of matter. This is why, on the sephirotic tree, Gabriel is the Archangel of Iesod, the region of the Moon. Unlike the Sun, which dilates, disperses and distributes, the Moon compresses, contracts and condenses. If it were not checked by other influences, it would petrify all life in plants, animals and humans.

Initiates, who are instructed in this science, try to use the period of the winter solstice to make their ideas and plans concrete, for this is the time when a birth takes place on earth. The other cardinal feasts correspond to other processes: Easter, to resurrection; St. John's day, to the kindling of fire; Michaelmas, to a stripping away. The feast of Christmas is linked to an incarnation, and this is why the birth of Christ, in the person of Jesus, has traditionally taken place in winter.

26 December

During the nine months spent in its mother's womb, a child is attached to its mother by the umbilical cord, and it therefore leads a life of dependency; it is the mother who breathes and eats for it. In the same way, until we have been born on the spiritual plane – what the Christian tradition calls the second birth – other beings eat and drink in our place and think in our place.

Humans leave their mother's womb, but they still live in another mother's womb: nature's. One day they will have to cut this umbilical cord, too, in order to become independent. In fact, even then they won't have completely gained their independence; there will be other cords to cut until the day they become as free as God. But that day is still far off, and, in the meantime, they must remain linked to their mother nature. Even if they reach higher regions, these are still nature, and they will still have cords to cut.

27 December

When we feel the need to merge with the universal soul, we contemplate the immensity of the sea or gaze at the multitude of stars in the boundless sky. But if we remained in this expanded, dispersed state, we would achieve nothing on earth; in order to act, we have to use the law of condensation, of concentration. We need vast spaces of sky or sea when we wish to expand, and then we need a very small space when we wish to concentrate and gather our forces.

Concentration and expansion correspond to the two astrological signs of Capricorn and Leo. Leo is a sign that externalizes: it projects and dispenses. Capricorn, on the other hand, is a sign that internalizes: it accumulates and condenses. Under its influence, between the months of December and January, the earth concentrates energies in the roots of trees in order to prepare for the explosion that takes place during the months of July and August, when an abundance of fruits appears under the influence of Leo.

28 December

Even if humans know very well what love is, they will never stop being interested in it. Why? Because, with love, it's not the intellectual side that counts: even if they know everything about love, this knowledge will not be enough for them. The only thing that matters is feeling, which is why the need to experience love is endless. You can know everything about love without ever tiring of feeling it. You could end up finding all other subjects boring some day; love is the only exception.

Take any other subject in life: as soon as you know it well, that's it, and you're not going to spend time on it for ever; once you've studied it, you put it to one side. But love is another matter; you will continue to be interested in it for eternity, because it's not an intellectual matter: whether you know it or not, you need to love and be loved. This is what makes love eternal.

29 December

Each day, learn to create an ideal image of yourself, for this image will help you in your spiritual work. Of course, you must not imagine you are already perfect, and above all you mustn't wish others to see you as such; otherwise, you will attract their mockery and hostility. They'll say, 'Who does he think he is? He's going mad!' And they won't be far wrong.

So, whatever inner work you have undertaken, continue to behave simply and naturally with others. Imagine that you are wise, luminous and radiant, that you are fulfilling God's will and that you're able to see yourself as the perfect being you were in the distant past, in the innocence and splendour of Paradise, and must once again be in the future. But, at the same time, remember it hasn't happened yet!

30 December

Two people meet. 'How are you doing?' 'Fine!' And if they know each other reasonably well, they embrace mechanically, out of habit. Then, since they're in a hurry, they leave each other, and they no longer even remember whether they embraced each other or not. They find nothing unusual about doing everything quickly, unconsciously, even embracing, and then they're surprised they don't receive much from their relationships with those they nevertheless call their friends.

You meet someone. Well, in the first place, you don't really need to embrace. But if you do, and even if you don't, put your thought and soul into this meeting for at least a few seconds, and its taste and perfume will linger and follow you for a long time to come.

31 December

In a few hours it will be New Year, and tomorrow when you speak about today you will already be saying 'last year'. Up until twenty-three hours, fifty-nine minutes and fifty-nine seconds, it will be 'this year', and as midnight strikes the new year will begin. One second, just one second, separates one year from the next! But there you are – you have to get to the last second. You have to pass through all the days of a year one after another to reach this last second.

Well, you should realize that this is how man's spiritual transformation takes place. In an instant he is totally renewed, regenerated. But it will have taken centuries and centuries of effort to arrive at this final moment. As with the old year, you will say of the period preceding this moment of regeneration, 'It was the old life', and as with the new year you will say of the new period that's dawning, 'This is the new life'. How long will you have to wait before you reach this final second? Don't worry about it; it will come for each and every person. So be patient; you have to know how to wait, but while you wait you must work.

There are five aspects to be studied in each Sephirah:

- *the name of God*
- *the name of the Sephirah*
- *the leader of the angelic order*
- *the angelic order*
- *the name of the planet*

    The Tree of Life is a symbolic figure which contains in condensed form the whole of initiatic science, the teachings of all initiates. It can be compared to a grain or seed; plant it and from it will spring creation and all created beings. This figure can be an extremely important pantacle, one of the most powerful instruments of magic that it is possible to have. It contains everything: all the principles, all the elements, all the factors with which God created the world.

    In the Tree of Life you have a system which can help you to avoid dispersing the efforts you devote to your spiritual work. If you work constantly with this figure for years, you will find that it brings order and balance to your life; everything within you will become organized and harmonious. Every time you have a moment to spare you can call to mind the Tree of Life and, by focusing on one Sephirah, strive to develop the qualities or energies it contains. Whatever you stand most in need of, be it light or love, strength, protection, generosity, justice, or life, look for it in the Tree of Life. The Tree of Life is there for us, for the sons and daughters of God who need to be nourished by divine life.

Omraam Mikhaël Aïvanhov
(The Fruits of the Tree of Life,
Complete Works, vol. 32, chap. 3)

TREE OF LIFE

1 Ehieh
Kether – *Crown*
Metatron
Hayoth haKadesch – *Seraphim*
Rashith haGalgalim – *First Swirlings (Neptune)*
♆

2 Yah
Chokmah – *Wisdom*
Raziel
Ophanim – *Cherubim*
Mazloth – *The Zodiac (Uranus)*
♅

4 El
Chesed – *Mercy*
Tzsadkiel
Hashmalim – *Dominations*
Tzedek – *Jupiter*
♃

3 Jehovah
Binah – *Understanding*
Tzaphkiel
Aralim – *Thrones*
Shabbathai – *Saturn*
♄

5 Elohim Gibor
Geburah – *Severity*
Kamaël
Seraphim – *Powers*
Maadim – *Mars*
♂

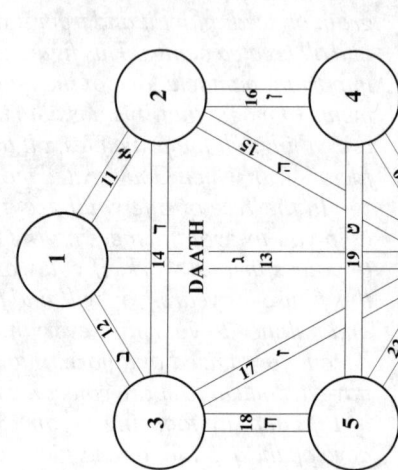

7 Jehovah Tzebaoth
Netzach – *Victory*
Haniel
Elohim – *Principalities*
Noga – *Venus*   ♀

6 Eloha vaDaath
Tiphareth – *Beauty*
Mikhaël
Malakhim – *Virtues*
Shemesh – *Sun*   ☉

8 Elohim Tsébaoth
Hod – *la Gloire*
Raphaël
Bneï-Elohim – *les Archanges*
Kohave – *Mercure*   ☿

9 Shaddai El Hai
Yesod – *Foundation*
Gabriel
Kerubim – *Angels*
Levana – *Moon*   ☽

10 Adonai-Melek
Malkuth – *The Kingdom*
Uriel (Sandalfon)
Ishim – *Beatified Souls*
Olem Ha Yesodoth – *Earth*
♁

Note: The three fundamental activities which characterize human beings are thinking (by means of the intellect or mind), feeling (by means of the heart), and doing (by means of the physical body). You must not believe that only the physical body is material; the heart and mind are also material instruments, but the matter of which they are made is far subtler than that of the physical body.

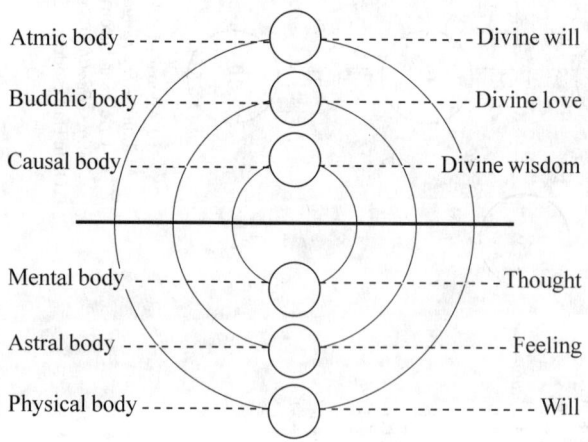

An age-old esoteric tradition teaches that the support or vehicle of feeling is the astral body, and that of the intellect, the mental body. But this trinity made up of our physical, astral, and mental bodies, constitutes our imperfect human nature, and the three faculties of thought, feeling, and action also exist on a higher level, their vehicles being respectively, the causal, buddhic, and atmic bodies which go to make up our divine self.

In the diagram, the three large concentric circles indicate the links which exist between the lower and the higher bodies. The physical body, which represents strength, will, and power on the material level, is linked to the atmic body, which represents divine power, strength, and will. The astral body, which represents our egotistical, personal feelings and desires, is linked to the buddhic body, which represents divine love. The mental body, which represents our ordinary, self-serving thoughts, is linked to the causal body, which represents divine wisdom.

(Man's Psychic Life: Elements and Structures,
Izvor Collection No. 222, chap. 3)

INDEX

A

Accusations, unjustified
- these push people to commit the faults of which they are accused, 18 Aug.

Action
- must be inspired by spiritual light, 21 July.

Advance, to
- is the law of life, 22 July.

Anarchy
- the state of those who don't devote their energies to serving a divine ideal, 8 Dec.

Angels
- their nature, 18 July.

Answers from God
- are inside us, 10 Dec.

Appreciation of heaven
- rely on heaven alone, 15 Sept.

Archangel Gabriel
- the transmission of genes, 21 Dec.

Archangel Michael
- separation, 29 Sept.

Archangel Raphael
- liberation of energies, 22 March.

Archangel Uriel
- reproduction, 21 June.

'Ask, and it will be given to you'
- commentary, 3 May.

Aspirations
- conditions for their realization, 21 April.

Attraction between people
- the origin, 24 Nov.

Awareness
- of weaknesses is the beginning of strength, 17 Feb.
- that takes place in the other world, 4 Oct.

B

Bee
- symbol of the initiate, 6 July.

Being born
- on the physical and spiritual planes: cords to cut, 26 Dec.

Bird
- symbol of the spiritualist, 24 Feb.

Birth
- fruit of love, 25 Oct.

Birth chart
- interpreted from the initiatic point of view, 4 Sept.

'Blessed are you when people revile you'
- commentary, 7 Oct.

Boredom
- the cause: an inability to feel the subtle side of life, 22 Nov.

Brotherhood
- ideal form of society, 26 July.

C

Capacity for endurance
- is the measure of our wisdom, 17 Aug.

Cells
- the usefulness of taming them, 6 Nov.

Changes
- depend on the efforts humans make to improve, 7 Nov.

Christmas
- feast of incarnation, 25 Dec.

Church
- must not maintain Christians in their illusions, 12 Feb.

Circle
- symbolism of the centre and of the periphery, 17 Nov.

Climb up to the spirit
- before descending into matter, 8 Oct.

Clouds
- rise above them to see the sun, 28 Nov.

Collective life
- the ideal to attain, 2 Aug.

Comfort
- harmful to our physical and psychic health, 27 March.

Comparisons
- beneficial and harmful, 9 July.

Concentration and expansion
- Capricorn and Leo, 27 Dec.

Consecration
- of your life to heaven, 5 Jan.

Considerations, social
- should mean little to us, 19 Sept.

Correcting a child
- precautions to take, 20 Nov.

Cosmic Man
- we live in him; moral consequences, 3 Jan.

Creation
- and formation, 20 June.

Cremation
- only suitable for very spiritual beings, 19 Jan.

Criterion
- for judging one's actions, 8 July.

Cross
- symbolism of the horizontal and the vertical, 29 Nov.

D

Dangers
- how to face them, 21 Feb.

Dark entities
- be aware of the danger they represent, 8 Aug.

Days of the week
- must all be considered holy, 19 March.

Dead, the
- you only find them again by cultivating the qualities you appreciated in them, 2 Nov.

Death
- on the spiritual plane, always followed by resurrection, 21 March.
- successive stages of awareness, 29 Oct.

Defences
- must be built every day, 2 March.

Desires
- ask yourself whether they conform to the divine laws, 16 Feb.

Difference
- what kind it's helpful to cultivate, 6 Sept.

Difficulties
- the attitude to face them with, 6 Oct.

Disillusionments
- must never make us lose our ideal, 14 Dec.

Divine origin
- we all bear traces of it within us, 1 July.

Divine presence
- is an inner state of consciousness, 8 Jan.

Divine right
- which we must defend in ourselves, 20 July.

Divine Word
- light is its first expression, 28 Oct.

Dream
- seed of all reality, 6 April.

E

Earth
- place where both good and evil are realized, 16 Jan.
- reacts to humans' behaviour, 12 July.
- its influence on human beings, 29 July.

Education
- true - is none other than initiation, 13 Dec.

Effort
- never give up, 1 Sept.

Emotions
- their effects on the physical body, 11 June.

Encounters
- with others: put your thought and awareness into them, 30 Dec.

Enemies
- the greatest victory: to transform them into friends, 20 Oct.

Entities
- dark and luminous ones within us; how to act towards them, 21 May.

Essential
- the life that's flowing today, 5 Nov.

Events in the universe
- are recorded in us, 9 Sept.

Everyday tasks
- while carrying them out, be aware of the realities of the divine world, 1 June.

Evil
- comes from not knowing how to deal with opposite poles, 19 Aug.

Evolution
- the ability to project oneself into the higher worlds, 27 Jan.
- law of life, 24 Sept.

Evolve
- to become conscious that we are part of a community, 23 Jan.

Evolving
- never stop enlarging the sphere of your concerns and activities, 11 Oct.

Experiences
- give preference to those that elevate you, 21 Aug.

External world
- will one day reflect the beauty of our inner world, 30 Nov.

F

Failures
- must not interrupt our ascent, 24 Dec.

Fear
- closes the doors of the kingdom of God to us, 16 Oct.
- we always have to confront it in its different forms, 6 Dec.

Fire
- of suffering and fire of divine love, 9 May.

Food
- by means of our thoughts and feelings we make it a source of energy, 2 Oct.
- is impregnated by our inner states, 2 July.

Forms
- are always broken up eventually, 3 June.
- preserve the old while preparing the new, 13 July.
- even a religion must change them, 28 July.

Four elements
- are a form of nourishment for us, 25 June.
- are food for us, 27 Nov.

Fraternal feeling
- must be the basis of human relationships, 24 Oct.

Freedom
- is only complete in our inner world, 3 March.
- is found in the world of the spirit, 24 May.
- merging with God, 4 July.
- submission to God's plans, 1 Oct.

Friendship and love
- implies trust, 8 June.

Full moon in May.
- work to be done during this period, 20 May.

Fundamental note
- which harmonizes all our contradictory tendencies, 21 Sept.

G

Glass half full
- and glass half empty; two philosophies, 10 Oct.

'Go, and do not sin any more'
- commentary, 27 Aug.

God
- it is he whom we love in human beings, 4 March.
- we have come from him and will return to him, 22 May.
- as he is our Father, we are of the same nature as him, 3 Dec.

'God is light within me'
- commentary on the Master Peter Deunov's formula, 3 July.

Gold
- puts us in touch with the sun, 13 Aug.

Good and evil
- spread in waves, 28 June.

Good imprints
- it's necessary to be very careful at the beginning, 27 May.

Good relationships
- conditions needed for them to last, 28 Jan.

Grain of gold
- placed within you by the Creator; make it grow, 30 March.

Great beings
- how to rediscover their traces, 7 July.

H

Habits
- links created with living entities, 24 April.

Hand
- our body and the universe are found in it, 18 Oct.

Happiness of others
- knowing how to rejoice in this is a sign of evolution, 5 Dec.

Harmony
- must be our primary concern, 16 Nov.

Heart-intellect-will
- instruments of our true victories, 12 April.

Heaven
- must not make us abandon the earth, 23 May.

Hedgehog
- symbolism, 30 Sept.

Height, depth, width
- how these correspond to human development, 31 Oct.

Help others
- by first gaining inner riches from God, 25 Jan.

High ideal
- gives meaning to our life, 27 Feb.

Higher Self
- seek it in the sun, 14 May.

Honesty
- does not justify saying whatever you please, 14 March.

Human being
- door of heaven or hell, 11 April.
- can be compared to a laboratory, 15 June.

Human respiration
- and cosmic respiration, 9 Jan.

I

'I am He'
- meaning of this saying 30 May.

'I am the light of the world'
- commentary, 29 May.

'I am the way, and the truth, and the life'
- commentary, 14 Jan.

'I walk before the Lord in the land of the living'
- commentary, 24 March.

Ideal self-image
- usefulness for spiritual work, 29 Dec.

'If salt has lost its taste…'
- commentary, 8 Nov.

Image of God
- we must use our gifts to find it inside, 19 Dec.

Immensity
- our soul's true homeland, 11 May.

Inertia
- of the heart and mind must be overcome, 19 Nov.

Influences
- it is always up to us whether we accept them or not, 13 Nov.

Inheritance
- must not be revealed until the heirs are worthy of it, 5 Feb.

Initiates
- summits that receive the first rays of the sun, 17 April.
- their greatness derives from overcoming their weaknesses, 15 May.

Initiatic Science
- essential for resisting life's traps, 21 Nov.

Initiatic teaching
- its programme, 10 Feb.

Initiation
- concerns the whole person, 13 Sept.
- takes place in everyday life, 22 Dec.

Injustices
- done to others: you participate when you do not oppose them, 23 Oct.

Inner enemies
- and outer enemies; how to deal with them, 1 May.

Inner experience
- alone gives us access to the divine world, 11 Jan.

Inner life
- a space we can constantly develop, 27 April.

Inner peace
- method to obtain it, 4 Jan.

Inner presence of people
- more important than their physical presence, 19 Oct.

Inner states
- attract currents of force from space which correspond to them, 9 Dec.

Inner world
- a way of getting in touch with it, 17 March.
- equip it well as we never stop living in it, 20 Dec.

J

Jesus
- came to fulfil the mission inscribed in his name, 15 Feb.
- is not the Christ, but he received the Christ, 16 April.

Justice
- defends mostly material interests, 9 Aug.

K

Kingdom of God and his justice
- working for it eclipses all other activity, 17 June.

Kingdoms
- from the mineral to the human, 11 Aug.

'Know thyself'
- commentary, 30 Oct.

Knowledge
- a fusion with what you want to know, 26 Sept.

L

Laboratories, inner
- better equipped than the scientists', 16 Sept.

Law of cause and effect
- is the foundation of justice, 15 Jan.

Laws of the earth
- no one is exempt from them, 26 April.

'Let him who is on the housetop not go down…'
Commentary, 3 Aug.

Life
- ceaselessly renewed in the cosmos, 25 March.
- sustain it by burning our impurities, 24 July.
- one continuous hierarchy, 23 Nov.
- know how to renew it in oneself so as to be always appreciated, 7 Dec.

Life on earth
- analogy with the stage, 26 Jan.

Lifting the veil of Isis
- interpretation, 28 March.

Light
- attract it and let it penetrate you, 10 Jan.
- enlightens our consciousness and protects us, 25 July.
- the greatest power, 23 Sept.

Links
- the circumstances in which they can be cut, 30 Aug.

Living nature
- make contact with it every morning, 16 July.

Love
- how to live it in order to receive it, 6 Jan.
- too often resembles theft, 17 Jan.
- if we nourish it with purity, it will never leave us again, 11 Feb.
- the work you have to do on yourself to attract it, 29 Feb.
- without waiting to be loved, 26 March.
- its highest manifestations, 8 April.

- live it as a state of consciousness, 5 May.
- learn to give and receive it, 15 July.
- exchanges between two energy currents, 30 July.
- with which we help our friends, 10 Aug.
- gives us the conviction we are immortal, 28 Aug.
- keep your distance so it may endure, 11 Sept.
- exchanges on the level of the soul and the spirit, 20 Sept.
- never speak of it to the person you love, 4 Nov.
- how it relates to water, wine and blood, 4 Dec.
- a subject we will never tire of, 28 Dec.

Love and wisdom
- know when to manifest them, 15 April.

Love God
- in order to give a solid foundation to our love for humans, 26 May.

Love of a person
- how to obtain it, 3 Oct.

Love of God
- is lived differently by different creatures, 8 Sept.
- gives us fulfilment and freedom, 17 Dec.

Luminous entities
- which link earth and heaven, 26 Oct.

Lyre
- symbol of the human being with their different bodies, 12 Jan.

M

Magic
- the science of influences, 5 June.
- founded on the law of correspondences, 23 June.
- the most powerful is found in the heart, 9 Oct.

Magical, the
- more real than reality, 23 Dec.

'Make love'
- commentary on this expression, 24 June.

Marriage
- union of spirit and matter, 30 June.

Masculine and feminine principles
- the effects when they meet, 25 April.

Material conditions
- never surrender to them, 21 Jan.

Materialistic philosophy
- cause of human blindness, 7 March.
- philosophy of appearances, 14 Sept.

Matter
- descend into it to give it life, 29 April.

Meals
- the meditation that must precede them, 24 Jan.
- opportunity to practise self-control, 9 April.

Mind
- its role in the work of the spirit on matter, 14 Aug.

Mission
- of souls who come to incarnate, 16 Dec.

Mistakes
- correct your own instead of pointing out other people's, 24 Aug.

N

Nature
- dangers of wishing to exploit it, 11 March.
- is alive and intelligent, 13 May.
- relate to all its inhabitants, 22 Sept.

New life
- passage from the old life to the new, 31 Dec.

New Year wishes
- 1 Jan.

Numbers
- the foundation of creation, 8 Feb.

Numbers 4 and 8
- symbolism and relationships, 10 May.

Nutrition
- concerns the whole of our being, 27 July.

O

Objects
- exorcise them before filling them with beneficial forces, 20 Feb.

Old age
- inevitable for the body but not for the heart, 5 July.

Opening up
- to receive life from everything around us, 22 Feb.

Ora et labora
- commentary, 4 Aug.

Ordeals
- do not wait for them to happen before seeking the means to deal with them, 19 April.
- in the life of an initiate, 13 June.

P

Parable of the pearl
- commentary, 3 Sept.

Patience
- reinforce it through breathing, 5 April.

Patience and impatience
- when to express them, 11 Dec.

Peace
- result of harmony between the different functions of our organism, 3 April.
- is first a state of consciousness, 23 Aug.

Penetrate
- beings and objects to act on them, 3 Nov.

Perfect yourself
- in order to give an example, 14 June.

Personal interests
- are not taken into account by true justice, 12 March.

Personal life
- is very little compared with the riches of universal life, 19 June.

Philosopher's stone
- 'woman's work and child's play', 22 Jan.
- it is in ourselves that we must look for it, 9 Nov.

Physical body
- make it a temple of the Lord, 23 April.
- it is given too much consideration at the expense of the soul and spirit, 14 July.
- reflection of divine virtues, 15 Oct.

Physical pain
- a warning, 5 March.

Physical remedies
- and spiritual remedies, 12 Dec.

Place
- that destiny reserves for us, 12 Oct.

'Place goodness as the base of your life'
- commentary, 16 May.

Plants
- their role in the refinement of matter, 26 June.

Pleasure
- natural tendency that must be controlled, 7 April.

Prana
- subtle energy we absorb during respiration, 13 April.

Prayer
- the spoken word supported by a thought and a feeling, 17 July.

Present
- consequence of the past, but also the starting point for a new life, 6 March.

Present life
- one stage in a long journey, 14 April.

Problems
- we must seek the solution

to them inside ourselves, 14 Feb.

Providence
- notion that is inspired by our faith in the spirit, 16 March.

Psychic difficulties
- mental exercise to neutralize them, 29 Jan.

Psychic pollution
- heightens the dangers of physical pollution, 11 July.

Public
- danger of compromising oneself to please them, 29 March.

R

Rebellion
- choose to direct it towards your inner enemies, 18 Nov.

Religion
- science of connection, in all areas, 8 March.
- too often reduced to dogmas and ritual, 23 July.

Responsibilities
- conditions for exercising them correctly, 28 Feb.

Resurrection
- analogy between human beings and the seed, 23 March.

Riches
- the most precious are buried deep within us, 26 Feb.
- discovered within through the desire to help others, 4 April.

Ritual
- is useful only if we give it a meaning; example of communion, 20 Jan.

Role models
- the ones needed are those who incarnate spiritual qualities, 31 May.

S

Sacred books
- do not solely contain truths that are irrefutable and for all time, 4 Feb.
- experience of higher worlds is needed to understand them, 12 June.

Sacrifice
- conditions for establishing good relationships with others, 28 May.

Sacrifices
- made through fraternal love: the only ones pleasing to God, 21 Oct.

Salt
- meditate on its origins and properties, 2 April.

Sanctity
- a state reached in full consciousness, 2 Jan.

School of life
- we will never leave it, 22 Aug.

Science and religion
- together must take account of the unity of the universe, 25 Sept.

Science of life
- opens us to the mysteries of Mother Nature, 19 July.

Scientific progress
- must direct spiritual evolution, 6 June.
- not enough to give meaning to life, 16 June.

'Seek first his kingdom and his righteousness'
- commentaries, 17 May.

Self-perfection
- increase the quality of vibrations, 8 May.

Sensations
- refine them and make them more intense, 26 Aug.

Sephirotic Tree
- work to make it bear fruit within us, 9 March.

Shift in consciousness
- exercise for changing one's inner states, 22 Oct.

Singers
- responsible for the way they use their voice, 12 May.

Social inequalities
- are explained by the law of reincarnation, 4 June.

Solar energy
- how it manifests in men and women; the sexual force, 25 Aug.

Solar plexus
- its function in our organism, 17 Oct.

Solutions
- to be found for each difficulty in life, 13 Jan.
- to problems; accept them even if they are difficult, 17 Sept.

Soul
- why it leaves the body during sleep, 12 Nov.

Specialists
- remove the object they are studying from the Tree of Life, 16 Aug.

Spirit
- must control all our activities, 20 Aug.
- restore it to its place at the centre, 26 Nov.

Spirit and matter
- 3 and 4, 14 Oct.

Spiritual brotherhood
- helps us to continue our efforts, 31 March.

Spiritual community
- its power, 25 May.

Spiritual life
- an ascent for which a guide is necessary, 7 May.

Spiritual master
- by revealing our weak points to us, he gives us the means to defend ourselves, 2 May.

Spiritual practice
- does not free you from all ills, 1 April.
- necessity for finding a more harmonious rhythm in life, 31 July.

Spiritual retreat
- strive to preserve its benefits, 27 Sept.

Spiritual work
- you must wait for its results, but they are lasting, 23 Feb.
- different ways of coming into contact with it, 20 April.
- an enterprise that never ends, 22 June.
- it is never too late to begin, 1 Nov.

Spiritualist séances
- a warning, 6 Feb.

Spirituality
- make the physical body the instrument of the spirit, 1 March.
- the main criterion is the light, 31 Jan.

Stability
- culminating point of initiation, 10 April.

Starry sky
- physical study and contemplation, 7 Aug.

Stones
- are living beings, 13 Oct.

Subject, verb, object
- God, angels, human beings, 19 Feb.

Suffering
- gives perfume and flavour to our life, 15 March.
- why heaven does not deliver us from it, 18 May.
- is only healed by wisdom and love, 27 Oct.
- of the spiritualist: freedom, 1 Dec.

Sulphur
- analogy with the intellect, 2 Feb.

Sulphur, mercury and salt
- transposed to our psychic life, 6 May.

Summit
- why you should address God himself, 31 Aug.

Sun
- symbol of the spirit, to which we must remain linked, 13 Feb.
- how to consider it, 19 May.

- symbol of the perfection Jesus asks us to seek, 9 June.
- why we must learn from the sun, 18 June.
- the ideal to be attained, 10 July.
- its lesson: there is only one religion, 15 Dec.

Support and understanding
- from the divine world must suffice us, 5 Oct.

Swamp
- an image of our difficulties, 18 Feb.

T

Taking and giving
- what motivates humans to leave their centre, 12 Sept.

Talents
- manifestations of spiritual entities within people, 25 Nov.

Technical progress
- its dangers for our inner development, 7 Jan.

Tenants
- in human beings, 14 Nov.

'The fear of the Lord is the beginning of wisdom'
- commentary, 15 Aug.

The Gospels
- are not applied, since they are not yet understood, 30 Jan.

Theoretical knowledge
- and knowledge that is lived, 18 Jan.

Thought
- instrument we must never abandon, 9 Feb.
- a means of gaining access to the divine world, 18 Sept.

Thoughts and feelings
- eventually alter the matter of the physical body, 10 June.

Thread, needle, cloth
- a human being's thought, will and body, 29 June.

Tree and river
- symbols of inner processes; example of love, 30 April.

Tree, and snake swallowing its own tail
- symbols of the unity of creation, 18 April.

Trials
- see the good they can bring, 7 Sept.
- prepare for them as you do for winter, 2 Dec.

Truth
- learn to appreciate it, whoever it comes from, 1 Feb.
- expression of unity, 25 Feb.
- finding it is an endless task demanding perseverance, 4 May.

- and nakedness, 5 Aug.
- eternal principle, which is very difficult to attain to, 10 Nov.

U

Unity
- condition of life, 27 June.

Universal Spirit
- sustains all creatures, 10 March.

Universal White Brotherhood
- its aim: to unite all people, 28 Sept.

V

Vigilance
- we must exercise it, especially within ourselves, 29 Aug.

Vision of the world
- depends on our state of consciousness; Nastradine Hodja, 10 Sept.

Visits
- by spirits from the invisible world, 1 Aug.

W

Walk, the way you
- study it in order to improve it, 7 June.

Wars
- ending them depends only on humans, 28 April.

Water
- teaches us two methods of purification, 2 June.
- symbolism of oxygen and hydrogen, 11 Nov.

Water and fire
- their cosmic dimension represented by the cross, 13 March.

Water, blood and light
- relationships between them, 20 March.

Waves
- travelling through space and through us, 5 Sept.

Will
- conditions for developing it, 6 Aug.
- instrument of our higher nature, 18 Dec.

Wisdom and love
- their role in the construction of our inner dwelling, 18 March.
- complementarity in action, 2 Sept.
- conditions of truth, 15 Nov.

Woman
- the educator of man, 7 Feb.

Wondrous country
- found within the human soul, 22 April.

Work
- our reason for being on earth, 3 Feb.
- for a divine idea brings fulfilment, 12 Aug.

Synopsis Collection

The Synopsis Collection offers a synthesis
of Omraam Mikhaël Aïvanhov's teaching

'You Are Gods'

Table of contents • **Part I - 'You Are Gods'** – 1. 'Be perfect as your heavenly Father is perfect' – 2. 'The Father and I are one' – 3. The return to the house of the Father • **Part II - What is human nature?** – 1. Lower nature and higher nature – 2. 'No one can serve two masters' I and II – 3. The three great temptations – 4. Taking and giving – 5. The voice of our higher nature – 6. Sensitivity to the divine world – 7. 'Blessed are the peacemakers' • **Part III - 'So God created humankind in his image'** – 1. God, nature, and humankind – 2. The Tree of Life – 3. From seed to tree – 4. The sun, image of God and image of humankind – 5. 'You shall love the Lord your God' • **Part IV - The laws of destiny** – 1. Laws of Nature and moral laws I. The law of cause and effect II. The law of recording III. The law of resonance IV. The law of affinity – 2. Reincarnation I. The teaching of the Gospels II. Making sense of fate III. We create our own future • **Part V - Answers to the question of evil** – 1. God transcends good and evil – 2. The only way to triumph over evil is to learn to use it – 3. 'Evil can be compared to tenants'• **Part VI - Spiritual alchemy** – 1. How to extract the quintessence – 2. The image of the tree. grafting – 3. The fire of sacrifice – 4. From movement to light : replacing pleasure with work – 5. Learn to eat and so learn to love • **Part VII - The organs of spiritual knowledge** – 1. The aura – 2. The solar plexus I. The solar plexus and the brain II. Oil in the lamp – 3. The Hara centre – 4. The Kundalini force and the chakras • **Part VIII - Living in eternal life** – 1. 'And this is eternal life, that they may know you, the only true God' – 2. 'Know Thyself' – 3. Merging with the cosmic Soul and Spirit • Part IX - The paths of divinization – 1. The feast of Christmas – 2. The second birth – 3. The resurrection and the last Judgement – 4. The body of glory • **Biblical references - Index**

By the same author

(Translated from the French)

Complete Works

- Volume 1 – The Second Birth
- Volume 2 – Spiritual Alchemy
- Volume 5 – Life Force
- Volume 6 – Harmony
- Volume 7 – The Mysteries of Yesod
- Volume 10 – The Splendour of Tiphareth
  The Yoga of the Sun
- Volume 11 – The Key to the Problems of Existence
- Volume 12 – Cosmic Moral Laws
- Volume 13 – A New Earth
  Methods, Exercises, Formulas, Prayers
- Volume 14 – Love and Sexuality (Part I)
- Volume 15 – Love and Sexuality (Part II)
- Volume 17 – 'Know Thyself' Jnana Yoga (Part I)
- Volume 18 – 'Know Thyself' Jnana Yoga (Part II)
- Volume 25 – A New Dawn: *Society and Politics in the Light of Initiatic Science (Part I)*
- Volume 26 – A New Dawn: *Society and Politics in the Light of Initiatic Science (Part II)*
- Volume 29 – On the Art of Teaching (Part III)
- Volume 30 – Life and Work in an Initiatic School
  Training for the Divine
- Volume 32 – The Fruits of the Tree of Life
  The Cabbalistic Tradition

Brochures:

- 301 – The New Year
- 302 – Meditation
- 303 – Respiration
- 304 – Death and the Life Beyond

Compact disc

CD5009AN – The Seed
CD5016AN – The Role of the Mother during Gestation *(2 CD)*

Videos (french/english)

V 4605 FR – V 4606 FR

By the same author
(Translated from the French)

Izvor Collection

201 – Toward a Solar Civilization
202 – Man, Master of his Destiny
203 – Education Begins Before Birth
204 – The Yoga of Nutrition
205 – Sexual Force or the Winged Dragon
206 – A Philosophy of Universality
207 – What is a Spiritual Master?
208 – Under the Dove, the Reign of Peace
209 – Christmas and Easter in the Initiatic Tradition
210 – The Tree of the Knowledge of Good and Evil
211 – Freedom, the Spirit Triumphant
212 – Light is a Living Spirit
213 – Man's Two Natures: Human and Divine
214 – Hope for the World: Spiritual Galvanoplasty
215 – The True Meaning of Christ's Teaching
216 – The Living Book of Nature
217 – New Light on the Gospels
218 – The Symbolic Language of Geometrical Figures
219 – Man's Subtle Bodies and Centres
220 – The Zodiac, Key to Man and to the Universe
221 – True Alchemy or the Quest for Perfection
222 – Man's Psychic Life: Elements and Structures
223 – Creation: Artistic and Spiritual
224 – The Powers of Thought
225 – Harmony and Health
226 – The Book of Divine Magic
227 – Golden Rules for Everyday Life
228 – Looking into the Invisible
229 – The Path of Silence
230 – The Book of Revelations: a Commentary
231 – The Seeds of Happiness
232 – The Mysteries of Fire and Water
233 – Youth: Creators of the Future
234 – Truth, Fruit of Wisdom and Love
235 – 'In Spirit and in Truth'
236 – Angels and other Mysteries of The Tree of Life
237 – Cosmic Balance, The Secret of Polarity
238 – The Faith That Moves Mountains
239 – Love Greater Than Faith
240 – Sons and Daughters of God

**World Wide - Editor-Distributor
Editions Prosveta S.A. - Z.A. Le Capitou - B.P. 12
F - 83601 Fréjus CEDEX (France)
Tel. (33) 04 94 19 33 33 – Fax (33) 04 94 19 33 34
Web: www.prosveta.com – e-mail: international@prosveta.com**

Distributors

AUSTRALIA
PROSVETA Australia
P.O. Box 538 – Mittagong – N.S.W. 2575 Australia
Tel. (61) (0) 2 4855 0189 – Fax. (61) (0) 2 4872 2641
e-mail: prosveta.au@bigpond.com

AUSTRIA
HARMONIEQUELL VERSAND – Hof 37 – A- 5302 Henndorf am Wallersee
Tel. / fax (43) 6214 7413 – e-mail: info@prosveta.at

BELGIUM & LUXEMBOURG
PROSVETA BENELUX – Beeldenmakersstraat 1 – B 8000 Brugge
Tel./Fax. (32)(0)50/61 69 10 – e-mail : prosveta@skynet.be
N.V. MAKLU Somersstraat 13-15 – B-2000 Antwerpen
Tel. (32) 3/231 29 00 – Fax (32) 3/233 26 59
S.D.L. CARAVELLE S.A. – rue du Pré aux Oies, 303 – 1130 Bruxelles
Tel. (32) 2 240 93 00 – Fax (32) 2 216 35 98
e-mail : info@sdlcaravelle.com

BULGARIA
SVETOGLED – Bd Saborny 16 A, appt 11 – 9000 Varna
e-mail: vassil100@abv.bg – Tel/Fax: (359) 52 63 90 94

CANADA
PROSVETA Inc. – 3950, Albert Mines – Canton-de-Hatley (Qc), J0B 2C0
Tel. (819) 564-8212 – Fax. (819) 564-1823
in Canada, call toll free: 1-800-854-8212
e-mail: prosveta@prosveta-canada.com / www.prosveta-canada.com

CONGO
PROSVETA CONGO
29, Avenue de la Révolution – B.P. 768 – Pointe-Noire
Tel. : (242) 948156 / (242) 5531254 – Fax : (242) 948156
e-mail: prosvetacongo@yahoo.fr

COLOMBIA
ASOCIACIÓN PROSVETA
Calle 146 Número 13 - 10, Apart. 404 Interior 2 – Cedritos – Bogotá, Colombia
Tel. (57-1) 6 14 53 85 – Fax. (57-1) 6 33 58 03 – Celular: (57) 311 8 10 25 42
e-mail: kalagiya@hotmail.com

CYPRUS
THE SOLAR CIVILISATION BOOKSHOP – BOOKBINDING
73 D Kallipoleos Avenue – Lycavitos – P. O. Box 24947, 1355 – Nicosia
e-mail: cypapach@cytanet.com.cy – Tel / Fax 00357-22-377503

CZECH REPUBLIC
PROSVETA – Ant. Sovy 18 – České Budejovice 370 05
Tel / Fax: (420) 38-53 10 227 – e-mail: prosveta@iol.cz

FRANCE – DOM TOM
   Editions Prosveta S.A. - B.P. 12 – F - 83601 Fréjus CEDEX (France)
   Tel. (33) 04 94 19 33 33 – Fax (33) 04 94 19 33 34
   e-mail: international@prosveta.com – www.prosveta.com

GERMANY
   PROSVETA Verlag GmbH – Heerstrasse 55 – 78628 Rottweil
   Tel. (49) 741-46551 – Fax. (49) 741-46552 – e-mail: prosveta7@aol.com

GREAT BRITAIN – IRELAND
   PROSVETA – The Doves Nest, Duddleswell Uckfield – East Sussex TN 22 3JJ
   Tel. (44) (01825) 712988 – Fax (44) (01825) 713386
   e-mail: prosveta@pavilion.co.uk

HAITI
   PROSVETA DÉPÔT HAITI – Angle rue Faustin 1er et rue Bois Patate #25 bis
   6110 Port-au-Prince – Haiti
   Tel. (509) 245 18 65 – Tel. (509) 464 80 88 – e-mail: rbaaudant@yahoo.com

HOLLAND
   STICHTING PROSVETA NEDERLAND
   Zeestraat 50 – 2042 LC Zandvoort
   Tel. (31) 33 25 345 75 – Fax. (31) 33 25 803 20
   e-mail: prosveta@worldonline.nl

ISRAEL
   Zohar, P.B. 1046, Netanya 42110 – e-mail: zohar7@012.net.il

ITALY
   PROSVETA Coop. a r.l.
   Casella Postale 55 – 06068 Tavernelle (PG)
   Tel. (39) 075-835 84 98 – Fax (39) 075-835 97 12 – e-mail: prosveta@tin.it

IVORY COAST
   Librairie Prosveta
   25 rue Paul Langevin Zone 4C – 01 Abidjan
   e-mail: prosvetafrique@yahoo.fr – Tel/Fax: (225) 21 25 42 11

LEBANON
   PROSVETA LIBAN – P.O. Box 90-995
   Jdeidet-el-Metn, Beirut – Tel. (03) 448560 – e-mail: prosveta_lb@terra.net.lb

NORWAY
   PROSVETA NORDEN – Postboks 318, N-1502 Moss
   Tel. (47) 69 26 51 40 – Fax (47) 69 26 51 08 – e-mail: info@prosveta.no

PORTUGAL
   EDIÇÕES PROSVETA
   Rua Palmira, 66 r/c - C – 1170 - 287 Lisboa
   Tel. / Fax (351) 213 540 764 – e-mail: prosvetapt@hotmail.com

ROMANIA
   ANTAR – Str. N. Constantinescu 10 – Bloc 16A - sc A - Apt. 9
   Sector 1 – 71253 Bucarest
   Tel. 004021-231 28 78 – Tel./ Fax 004021-231 37 19
   e-mail : prosveta_ro@yahoo.com

RUSSIA
   EDITIONS PROSVETA
   143 964 Moskovskaya oblast, g. Reutov – 4, post/box 4
   Tel./ Fax. (095) 525 18 17 – Tel. (095) 795 70 74
   e-mail: prosveta@online.ru

SPAIN
 ASOCIACIÓN PROSVETA ESPAÑOLA – C/ Ausias March n° 23 Ático
 SP-08010 Barcelona – Tel (34) (93) 412 31 85 – Fax (34) (93) 318 89 01
 e-mail: aprosveta@prosveta.es

UNITED STATES
 PROSVETA US Dist.
 26450 Ruether Ave #205 – Santa Clarita CA 91350
 Tel. (661) 251-5412 – Fax. (661) 252-1751
 e-mail: prosveta-usa@earthlink.net. / www.prosveta-usa.com

SWITZERLAND
 PROSVETA Société Coopérative
 Ch. de la Céramone 2 – CH - 1808 Les Monts-de-Corsier
 Tel. (41) 21 921 92 18 – Fax. (41) 21 922 92 04
 e-mail: prosveta@bluewin.ch

VENEZUELA
 PROSVETA VENEZUELA C. A. – Calle Madrid
 Edificio La Trinidad – Las Mercedes – Caracas D.F.
 Tel. (58) 414 134 75 34 – e-mail: prosvetavenezuela@gmail.com

Updated list 04.05.07 If you cannot contact one of these distributors, consult the internet site www.prosveta.com

---

The aim of the Universal White Brotherhood association
is the study and practice of the Teaching
of Master Omraam Mikhaël Aïvanhov,
published and distributed
by Prosveta.

All enquiries about the association should be addressed to:
Universal White Brotherhood
The Doves Nest, Duddleswell, Uckfield
East Sussex TN22 3JJ, GREAT BRITAIN
Tel: (44) (0)1825 712150 – Fax: (44) (0)1825 713386
E-mail: uwb@pavilion.co.uk

Printed in June 2007
by GRAFICA VENETA S.p.A.
Via Padova, 2 – 35010 Trebaseleghe (PD) – Italy

Dépôt légal : Juin 2007